BARRON'S

HOW TO PREPARE FOR THE

U.S. CITIZENSHIP TEST

5TH EDITION

BARRON'S

HOW TO PREPARE FOR THE

U.S. CITIZENSHIP TEST

5TH EDITION

Gladys Alesi, M.B.A.
Executive Director
American Immigration and Citizenship Conference

Formerly Administrator of English and
Citizenship Program of
New York City Board of Education

BARRON'S

All inquiries should be addressed to:
Barron's Educational Series, Inc.
250 Wireless Boulevard
Hauppauge, New York 11788
http://www.barronseduc.com

Library of Congress Catalog Card No. 99-32624
International Standard Book No. 0-7641-0767-4

Library of Congress Cataloging-in-Publication Data

Alesi, Gladys E.
    How to prepare for the U.S. citizenship test / by Gladys Alesi.—
5th ed.
        p.   cm.
    Includes bibliographical references and index.
    ISBN 0-7641-0767-4
    1. Citizenship—United States Examinations, questions, etc.
I. Title.   II. Title: U.S. citizenship test.
JK1758.A62   2000   99-32624
323.6'23'0973—dc21   CIP

Printed in the United States of America
9

Contents

List of Charts and Illustrations vii
Foreword viii
Acknowledgments ix
A Letter from the Author ix
Important Note x
Instructions to a Helper x
Basic Instructions for Using This Book xi
Quiz xii
Read About Tests xii

PART ONE—ARE YOU READY?

The Pretest 3
   Questions About Local Government 5
   Now, Read This 6
Looking Ahead 7
   The Flag 8
The Steps: Alien to Citizen 9
Reading Practice 11
   1. What Citizenship Means 11
   2. What Naturalization Means 13
   3. Immigration 15
   4. Rights of Citizens 17
   5. Responsibilities of Citizens 19
   6. Exceptions to Some Requirements for Citizenship ... 21
   7. Summary: How to Move from Alien to Citizen 22

PART TWO—YOU ARE READY!

Climbing the Steps—An Introduction 25
   Who Can Apply? 25
   Getting Started 26

STEP 1—How to Begin   **27**

Forms and Fees   27
Some Questions You May Have   54

STEP 2—Filing Your Form   **57**

Form N-400: Now Fill Out the Real Thing   57
Probability Questions   64

STEP 3—Serious Study   **67**

Practice Test of Written English   68
Reading Practice I   71
Reading Practice II   73
Reading Practice III   75
Review: More Writing Practice   76

STEP 4—Serious Study—History and Civics   **77**

Our Government   78
The Constitution: A Law for All Seasons   80
Reading Practice   85
Summary: How the Bill of Rights Protects Americans   86
The Federal Government: Form and Structure   87
State and Local Governments   99
The Declaration of Independence   104
The American Flag   107
The Final Test   109

STEP 5—The Naturalization Interview and the Oath   **113**

Review of the Steps to Citizenship   115
Review of the Probability Questions   116

APPENDIX—For Ready Reference   **119**

American English: Idiomatic Expressions   121
American English: Pronunciation Practice   127
National Holidays   129
Special Observances   131
The Declaration of Independence   133
The Constitution   137
A Look at American History   148
Immigration Update   187
Sample Completed Form N-400   191
Word List   197
Answer Key   209
Index   215

LIST OF CHARTS AND ILLUSTRATIONS

1 America Is Her Flag   8
2 Some of Our First Immigrants   16
3 Some Important Rights Under the Constitution   18
4 Application to File Declaration of Intention Form N-300   29
5 Application for Naturalization Form N-400   31
6 Application for Permanent Residence Form I-485   35
7 Form I-485 Supplement A   39
8 Additional Questions to Be Completed by All Applicants for Permanent Residence in the United States Form 9003   41
9 Biographic Information Form G-325A   42
10 Application for New Naturalization or Citizenship Paper Form N-565   43
11 Application to Replace Alien Registration Card Form I-90   46
12 Petition for Alien Relative Form I-130   47
13 Application for Voluntary Departure Under the Family Unity Program Form I-817   50
14 The Voters of the United States Elect   79
15 The Constitution as It Was Adopted   81
16 The Bill of Rights—1791   82
17 Amendments Passed After the Bill of Rights   83
18 Four Ways of Amending Our Federal Constitution   84
19 A Tripartite System—The Principle of Checks and Balances in Our Government   89
20 How a Bill Becomes a Law   91
21 Executive Branch of Our Federal Government   92
22 The President   93
23 Judicial Branch of Our Federal Government   97
24 How the Organization of Government in Cities, States, and the Nation Is Much Alike   101
25 Delegated Powers in the Federal System   102
26 The Federal System   103
27 The Liberty Bell   106
28 Sample Completed Form N-400   192

Map: The United States of America—The Present   219
Map: The United States of America—A Historical Perspective   220

Foreword

This book is a complete guide to citizenship in the United States. Any permanent resident who wants to become an American citizen through naturalization will find it easy to use this guide. An alien can use this comprehensive book to become a citizen if he or she meets the requirements of the latest immigration law as outlined here. All of the steps that need to be taken are explained in this book.

Following these steps is easy, but they must be done exactly. The sample questions must be practiced, and the reading exercises must be done. A person who wants to become a citizen must understand that this work is necessary and worthwhile.

The book is divided into two parts:

Part One: Are You Ready? This section contains a Pretest to determine readiness.

Part Two: You Are Ready! This section provides the information needed to start the naturalization process. The Appendix contains a review of American history and government. All of the important documents are there. Sample questions on them are included, as well as sample forms all filled out to show how they should look.

This book is about naturalization, the process by which people born in other countries become citizens of the United States. Being a citizen means being a part of our government. Only citizens have the right to vote and, thus, to choose the people who run the government. Citizens respect and support their government.

The final naturalization ceremony takes place in court. It is an exciting experience. When you step into the courtroom you are an alien, or stranger, but when you step out, after you have been naturalized, you are a citizen! You have full rights as an American citizen, the same rights and privileges as a person who was born in the United States. You can look to the government to protect you and your rights.

Do not ask anyone to translate this book for you. You will lose all the benefit of direct practice in your new language! Use a dictionary to help you with the difficult words. You will remember the words better if *you* look them up in your own dictionary. Help yourself to citizenship!

Acknowledgments

The author gratefully acknowledges the kindness of those concerned with granting permission to reprint passages, charts, and drawings. Special appreciation is offered to the U.S. Department of Justice, whose descriptive drawings, charts, and vocabulary test (which has been expanded and adapted) have helped to enhance this publication. Acknowledgment is also given for:

Sections on the chronological table of events in American history: *Nelson Klose and David Midgley,* American History at a Glance, © *1988, 1983* *Barron's Educational Series, Inc., Hauppauge, New York.*

A Letter from the Author

Dear Reader,

For many years, I taught citizenship to newcomers. I went with many of my students to their naturalization hearings. I heard the words of welcome spoken by officials. These experiences are the basis for my book. I know it will help you to go from alien to citizen. It is all you need to study.

This book is in simple English, the kind you need for your examination. Do not translate into your native language as you go along because that will only take you longer to learn what you need to study. Don't think you are helping yourself by reading instructions in your native language. I have worked with students and I know. Read each lesson aloud even if at first you find it difficult to say some of the words. Practice in front of a mirror. If you have a friend or relative to work with you, show that person this book.

Walk proudly as a new American in this nation of immigrants! Help yourself to citizenship so that you are really a part of your new country! Start today. You can do it!

Most sincerely,

Gladys Alesi

Gladys Alesi

Important Note

All of the preparation materials in this book are in accordance with present immigration law. At this time (1999) changes are being contemplated by the United States Congress. Because changes are possible, it is important to check with the INS office for the most current information. If you are affected by these changes, it is best to consult an immigration attorney.

Instructions to a Helper

Citizenship is a great prize won by thousands of people every year. If you are helping someone achieve citizenship, do the following:

1. Listen and praise good work.
2. Encourage the person to use English.
3. Make minimal corrections, but do not translate whole paragraphs, or even complete sentences. Have the person use the Word List.

This book involves a great deal of repetition. What may seem boring is necessary. Let the applicant ask the questions and give the answers aloud in order to become familiar with the sounds of English. Make it fun!

The end of this book contains a detailed history that is for reference only.

Basic Instructions for Using This Book

Read this section aloud to a friend or in front of a mirror:
I am *eligible* for naturalization because I meet these requirements:

1. I am 18 years old or older.
2. I was legally admitted for permanent residence or I applied for legalization, according to the Immigration Reform and Control Act of 1986.
3. I have resided here for at least five years, unless I qualify for an exception (see page 21).
4. I am a person of good moral character.

And I am learning to read, write, and speak English as I am gaining knowledge of the fundamentals of American history and government. Working with this book and practicing the exercises regularly will help me achieve my goal.

This book has two parts. Here is a short summary:

PART ONE

Basics—a Pretest to show you where you are right now. If you pass this test, you are ready to file your application. If you do not pass, do not feel bad, just continue the reading exercises. Put a line (___) under words you do not understand, and look them up in the Word List on page 197. You will soon be ready!

Practice in using citizenship words and ideas. Do all of the reading exercises! You are getting better already! Do the pretest again! This time, enter the answers on a separate sheet of paper. You should have gotten more correct this time. Now begin PART TWO, which follows:

PART TWO

Step 1: Applying for naturalization—forms and fees.
Step 2: Filing your forms.
Step 3: Serious study of English—reading and writing practice.
Step 4: Serious study of history and civics—more reading practice and the final test. Check your answers. If you made some errors, repeat those questions. Be sure to read this unit more than once. It is your key to success.
Step 5: The naturalization interview and the oath. Review the probability questions that the interviewer may ask.

Quiz

Read these questions and write the answers on the lines.

1. How many parts are in this book? _____

2. What is a pretest? _____

   _____

3. Which section will help you with written English? _____

   _____

4. Which section will tell about our government and history? _____

   _____

5. Which section will tell you about the interview? _____

   _____

Check your answers before going on to Part One.
(Turn the book upside down to find the correct answers.)

Read About Tests

There are many tests in this book. They provide the practice you need. Another word for test is *quiz*. Some of the short tests are called *reviews*. A review means "a systematic study of something just learned." Halfway through this book, you will find *progress tests*. Take all of them, even those that seem difficult at first. You will gain confidence as you do them again and again. Look ahead to the time you can discuss them as a citizen!

Now go to Part One. Take a very important test—the Pretest. Read it first. Then write the answers. Go to page 3, now.

Answers
1. Two
2. A test given before instruction
3. Part Two, Step 3
4. Step 4
5. Step 5

PART ONE

★★★★★★★★★★★★★★★★★★★★★★★★

Are You Ready?

The Pretest

*P*re means before. This test is called a Pretest because it is taken *before* you begin the steps to citizenship. It also tells how well you can answer the questions about yourself right now.

This test should give you an idea of how well you are prepared for your citizenship test and what you need to study. See how well you do. If you do well, it should not take long for you to prepare for the test. If you don't do well, do not be concerned. The following units will help you become prepared.

For each of the questions, write the answer in the space provided.

1. What is your family name? (last name) _____

   _____

2. What is your given name? (first name) _____

   _____

3. Where do you live now? (city/state) _____

   _____

4. Where were you born? _____

   _____

5. When were you born? (month/day/year) _____

   _____

6. What state do you live in? _____

   _____

The answers to questions 7 through 15 are listed below. Find the correct answer for each question and write the word in the space provided.

governor
legislative, executive, judicial
Constitution
vote
president

50
Congress
Supreme Court
democracy

7. How many states are in the United States? _____

_____

8. What form of government does the United States have? _____

_____

9. Who makes the laws for the country? _____

_____

10. What are the three branches of the government? _____

_____

11. What is the supreme law of the land? _____

_____

12. What is the highest court in the United States? _____

_____

13. What is the title of the chief executive of the United States government? _____

_____

14. What is the title of the chief executive of the state government? __

_____

15. What can a citizen do that an alien cannot? _____

_____

Now answer these questions:

16. What are the colors of the American flag? _____

_____

Are You Ready?

17. What do the colors stand for? _____

_____

18. How many stripes are in the flag? _____

_____

19. How many stars are in the flag? _____

_____

20. What is the national anthem (song)? _____

_____

The answers to questions 7 through 20 are on page 209. If you had 10 correct answers, you passed this test.

Questions About Local Government

Ask a neighbor or your helper to give you the answers to these 5 questions. Write the answers down in block letters like this: GLADYS ALESI. Review them again and again. Tear out this sheet or copy both the questions and their answers on a separate sheet of paper.

1. What congressional district do you live in? _____

_____

2. What is the name of your congressman or congresswoman? _____

_____

3. What are the two main political parties? _____

_____

4. Who are the two senators from your state? _____

_____

5. What political parties do these three elected officials represent? __

_____

It is important that you know the names of your representatives. The naturalization examiner sometimes asks them. It is easy if you are prepared and if you can say their names in understandable speech!

Now practice printing your name.

What is your full and correct name?_____
(Print your first name first.)

If you have ever used a different name, write it here. _____

> End of Pretest.

Now, Read This

You have completed the Pretest. You checked your answers with those on page 209. How many correct answers did you have? Ten? That is good! You have passed the first test!

You may begin Part Two now. Go to page 25 now!

If you did not pass the Pretest, do not worry. Do all of the reading exercises in Part One. Take the Pretest once more. This time, write the answers on a sheet of plain paper and check them with the answers on page 209. You may have them all right now! Follow this procedure as many times as you need, for you are working toward your goal—passing the test!

There are many tests in this book. They provide the practice you need. Another word for test is *quiz*, and still another is *review*. A review means a systematic study of something just learned, and that is an important way to study.

Take all of the tests in the book. You will gain confidence as you do more and more of them.

Look ahead to the time when you will become a citizen!

Looking Ahead is the title of the next page. Read it out loud.

Looking Ahead

The Pretest showed you some of the things you need to know. You also need to improve your English language skills. You can do this at the same time as you learn about the government and history of your new country, that is, if you follow all the instructions. You will be given reviews so that you are well prepared when the time comes for you to take the Oath of Allegiance to your new country!

Think what it will be like when you have your citizenship papers! Or, when you ask a neighbor, for the first time, "Where do I go to vote?" You can look forward to that if you follow the steps to citizenship in this book. You can do it! It may seem long and difficult but time passes quickly when you take the steps.

Practice makes perfect! That old saying tells you how to do it. Reading and answering questions about what you have read will help. Get a local newspaper to read, and try to make up your own questions about what you have read. Put a line under words you don't understand. Find out what they mean by asking a neighbor, by looking up the word in the Word List at the back of this book, or by using a dictionary. Most important, take all of the tests in this section. Whenever you can, read them out loud. Do each exercise several times. Follow the instructions each step of the way.

Now, turn the page and read about the American flag. Answer the questions about it. You may hear a question about the flag at your naturalization examination. You are looking ahead to American citizenship—it takes time and work. Take the first step.

The Flag

Another word for flag is *banner*. The national anthem is the "Star-Spangled Banner." Sometimes the flag is called Old Glory.

Would you have been able to answer questions 16–20 on the Pretest if you had read the following poem? Read it aloud now.

America Is Her Flag

Fifty stars are in her flag
for the 50 states in her Union.
June 14, 1777, the flag of the United States of America
had 13 stars—one for each state in the new Union.

This flag had 13 stripes,
a ribbon for each of the first colonies.

And poets say the colors in our flag
stand for the things we hold dear—
red for courage,
white for truth,
blue for honor.

A country is as strong as its ideals.

We love the things for which Old Glory stands.

You can help hold these colors high.

Figure 1

Source: U.S. Department of Justice, Immigration and Naturalization Service

The Steps:
Alien to Citizen

For immigration purposes, you are an *alien* if you are not a citizen of the United States, if you are a citizen of another country, or if you are stateless (without a country). As an alien, you may be an immigrant (if you want to live here permanently) or you may be a nonimmigrant (if you came here for a special purpose). There are many different kinds of nonimmigrants, but here we are concerned with aliens who are lawfully admitted immigrants.

There are four different kinds of immigrants: preference immigrants, special immigrants, immediate relatives of U.S. citizens, and refugees. There are six different kinds of preference immigrants—the first two being unmarried children of citizens, and spouses and unmarried children of permanent resident aliens. More about this later.

An immigrant may become a citizen through naturalization. The Immigration and Naturalization Service (INS) of the U.S. Department of Justice is in charge.

Under the law, an alien must file an application (Form N-400) to the INS. A sample form, all filled out, is on page 192. This is the first step.

The second step involves getting a letter from the INS telling the person to come to an office on a certain date for an interview.

The third step is the interview itself.

The fourth step is a naturalization ceremony, where the applicant takes the oath of allegiance and becomes a citizen.

Reading Practice

Y ou have read some general information about citizenship in the United States. In this unit, you will again read some of the same information, broken down into exercises for reading comprehension. The contents of this section will prepare you for the job to be done when you apply for citizenship.

There are six reading exercises and a summary in this unit. Do them in order—the first, second, and so on—answering the questions before you go to the next passage. Check your answers with those on pages 209–210. Do not give up until they are all correct!

Now, begin with reading exercise 1. Follow instructions. Read out loud.

1. What Citizenship Means

Do you know what a citizen is? A **citizen** is a part of his or her country. In the United States, a citizen is a free man or woman—free to make choices and free to help pick the people who govern. The opposite of a citizen is an **alien,** or stranger. You want to become a citizen! A person who likes the business he or she works for may want to become a partner, but it is not always easy to become a partner in a business. The United States government, however, makes it easy for you to become a partner in *its* business.

A citizen has many rights. The most important one is the right to vote. A citizen can vote in national, state, and local elections. A citizen helps to decide who will be president of the United States and who will make the laws for the nation, state, and city. A citizen can also vote for the local school board, the group of men and women who decide on the policies for the public schools.

There are other rights. For example, certain jobs are open only to citizens. These are often civil service jobs that offer security and many benefits. There is no question of a citizen's legal rights to receive Social Security payments in later life or to obtain welfare if needed. American citizens with American passports are free to travel all over the world. Citizens do not have to report changes of address to the attorney general within 10 days of occurrence, as aliens must.

To sum up, a citizen belongs. But nothing in life comes free. There are costs to be shared. Yes, there is a price, but the price is right! You will learn what that price is.

REVIEW

Do you know what these words mean? Write the meaning next to each word. If you are not sure, look up the meaning in the Word List at the end of this book.

1. alien _____

2. citizen _____

3. democracy _____

4. security _____

5. benefit _____

Now read the following questions. Write the answers in the spaces provided.

6. The opposite of *right* is *wrong*.

   a. What is the opposite of *citizen*? _____

   _____

   b. What is the opposite of *difficult*? _____

   _____

7. Is it easy or difficult to become a citizen? _____

   _____

8. Do you want to be a citizen or an alien? _____

   _____

9. What are some of the benefits of citizenship? _____

   _____

   _____

10. What are some of the rights of a citizen that you want to have?___

   _____

   _____

Check your answers with the answer key on page 209.

2. What Naturalization Means

Naturalization includes the word *natural* and it means giving an alien (or foreign-born person) the rights and privileges of a natural-born citizen.

Naturalization means taking certain steps set by law to become a citizen. These steps are petitioning or asking for citizenship, proving eligibility and residence here, and taking the Oath of Allegiance (a promise of loyalty) to the United States of America.

Look at the people you meet on the job, in your neighborhood, at school, and in government offices. Most of them are citizens. Some of them were born here; others were **naturalized.** These others came here as strangers or immigrants and became citizens by naturalization.

Immigrants are people who enter the country for the purpose of living here. We are a nation of immigrants, as President John F. Kennedy told us in his book of that title. He said that the first settlers who came to this country in the 16th century and those who come today, wanting to live here, are all immigrants or the children of immigrants!

Another president, George Bush, said that America's greatness was "forged (created) by the talents, the hard work, and the hopes of people who came to our shores." He said that at a naturalization ceremony on Citizenship Day, September 17, 1988, before he became president.

"Welcome, new Americans," those are the words that open the naturalization ceremony. You will also hear those words when you are sworn in. You may also hear something like this: "Be proud of your roots, love the places where you have lived, and be proud of your success in attaining citizenship!"

Recent immigrants have had help from the Immigration Reform and Control Act of 1986 and the Immigration Act of 1990. Among them have been refugees, people who can never go home again. They benefited from the Refugee Act of 1980. This law allowed people who were persecuted, or who have a well-founded fear of persecution on account of race, religion, or political opinion, to enter the United States of America.

All of these people are welcomed here. They go through the same steps to naturalization as you will. And you will become a citizen as earlier immigrants did, with the important rights of a natural-born American citizen!

Let us look at the last step in the naturalization process. You are in a large courtroom in front of a judge. Perhaps, as in a big city, there are many other people there, too. Some of your friends and relatives may be there, sitting on the benches behind you.

The clerk of the court says the words of the Oath of Allegiance. You repeat the words. In brief, they say that you will be loyal to the Constitution and laws of the United States of America. That is what you swear to do.

Other people who by law must take oaths like this one are the president and vice president, as well as many high government officials. The oath ends with the words, *So help me, God!*

After taking this oath, you are an American citizen. You will receive your Certificate of Naturalization (citizenship papers) by mail. But even before you do, you have all the benefits of citizenship.

Now you are not an alien or stranger, but a part of this country! You can vote, run for office, and be elected to all positions except two: the president and vice president of the United States of America.

You have read about the last step in the naturalization process. In Part Two you will start at the beginning and find out what the first step is. But first, do the review exercise on this page. And read passages 3, 4, 5, 6, and 7.

REVIEW

Do you know what these words mean? Write the meaning next to each word. If you are not sure, look up the meanings in the Word List at the end of this book.

1. naturalized _____

2. settle _____

3. immigrant _____

4. refugee _____

5. oath _____

6. allegiance _____

7. persecution _____

8. political opinion _____

Now, write the answers to the following questions in the space provided.

9. Where does naturalization take place? _____

_____

10. What is the Oath of Allegiance? _____

_____

11. Why do you want to become a citizen of the United States?_____

_____

12. Can a naturalized citizen become a U.S. Senator, a mayor, a governor?_____

_____

13. Can a naturalized citizen become president of the United States (or vice president)? _____

_____

See the answer key on page 209.

4. Rights of Citizens

The Constitution is the supreme, or highest, law of the United States. It was written a long time ago and became the law of the land for the United States of America in 1789. Since that time, it has been changed, or **amended,** 27 times. This means that there are 27 amendments to the Constitution of the United States of America. The Fourteenth Amendment states the rights of citizens, as follows:

> *All persons born or naturalized in the United States, and subject to the <u>jurisdiction</u> thereof, are citizens of the United States and of the State <u>wherein they reside.</u> No state shall make or enforce any law which shall <u>abridge</u> the privileges or <u>immunities</u> of citizens of the United States; nor shall any State <u>deprive</u> any person of life, liberty, or property, without due process of law; nor deny to any person within its <u>jurisdiction</u> the equal protection of the laws.*

Because these are our most important rights, it is important to state them in simple English:

> *All persons born or naturalized in the United States, and living here under U.S. law, are citizens of the United States and of the state in which they live (<u>reside</u>). No state can make or carry out a law that limits (<u>abridges</u>) a citizen's Constitutional privileges or freedom. And no state can take away (<u>deprive</u>) life, liberty, or property without following fixed legal rules and procedures. All citizens are to be treated equally under the law and are entitled to the same protection within each state. Wherever a citizen travels, he or she is protected by the United States of America.*

A citizen has a voice in the government. Only a citizen can vote for the officials who make the rules under which he or she lives, and only a citizen can hold office if elected. A citizen may work for the government under civil service.

REVIEW

you know what these words mean? Write the meanings next to the words. If are not sure, look up the meaning in the Word List at the end of the book.

1. amendment_____

2. jurisdiction _____

3. residence _____

4. abridge_____

SOME IMPORTANT RIGHTS UNDER THE CONSTITUTION

Freedom of Speech

The Constitution

Freedom of Worship

Right to Petition the Government

Freedom of the Press

Right to a Fair Trial

Freedom to Meet Peaceably

Right to Hold Property

Right to Life and Liberty

Figure 3

Source: U.S. Department of Justice, Immigration and Naturalization Service

5. immunity _____

6. deprive _____

Now write the answers to the following questions in the spaces provided.

7. What is the highest law of the land? _____

_____

8. How many amendments are there? _____

_____

9. Which amendment tells about the rights of citizens? _____

_____

10. Can you tell what these rights are? _____

_____

11. Which of the rights is the most important to you? _____

_____

See the answer key on page 210.

5. Responsibilities of Citizens

We said before that citizenship has many benefits and that all citizens must pay for these benefits. We also said that the price was right.

There is a Spanish proverb that tells us to "take what we want and pay for it." We have made a choice. We have chosen to become citizens. Now we must pay for that choice. We must register to vote and then vote on Election Day. We must work with others to make this a better place in which to live. Our government is a **democracy.** This means that through our vote we have a voice in government. We also have the right to join a political party. In doing so, we join with others who feel as we do.

Knowing all you can about the issues and keeping up-to-date on what is going on in your country are other responsibilities. The quality of government is improved when voters know who the candidates for office are. Governments don't run by themselves.

When persons are tried for criminal or civil offenses, they are often judged guilty or innocent by a jury of their peers. This means that people who are citizens have to be willing to give their time to serve on a jury. When you become a citizen, you may be called for jury duty. One of the prices of citizenship is to be willing to serve if you are called. You will not be called more than once a year.

We can say that the price of citizenship includes doing the following:

- Keeping informed about what is going on
- Voting in every election
- Obeying the laws
- Paying taxes
- Defending the country if it becomes necessary*
- Serving on a jury if called
- Being willing to hold office

QUIZ

Do you know what these words mean? Write the meanings next to the words. If you are not sure, look them up in the Word List at the end of the book.

1. benefit _____

2. democracy _____

3. responsibility _____

4. informed _____

5. criminal _____

6. civil _____

7. jury _____

Now write the answers to these questions in the space provided.

8. Are all the benefits of citizenship free? _____
_____

9. What is the price of citizenship? _____
_____

10. Why should a citizen vote? _____
_____

11. Why should a citizen serve on a jury? _____
_____

12. What are the responsibilities of citizenship? _____
_____

See the answer key on page 210.

---

*If it is not against your religion to do so.

6. Exceptions to Some Requirements for Citizenship

In reviewing the main requirements for naturalization (see p. xi), note that there are some *exceptions*. For example:

Item 2—You must have been legally admitted to the United States for permanent residence. The amnesty law passed in 1986 helps former illegal aliens to establish lawful permanent residence. (See section on Immigration Update.)

Item 3—You must have been a legal resident of the United States continuously for at least five years. Some exceptions to this rule are wives, husbands, or children of citizens, or persons in the armed forces or navy.

Item 4—You must understand English and be able to read, write, and speak ordinary English. One exception to this rule is an applicant who is older than 50 years old and has lived in the United States for at least 20 years.

Item 5—You must have a knowledge and understanding of the history and government of the United States. An applicant who has a physical or developmental disability or a mental impairment may be eligible for an exception to this requirement.

However, there are no exceptions from the requirement that you must take the Oath of Allegiance to the United States. If you cannot take and understand the meaning of the oath, you are not eligible for citizenship.

Answer the quiz that follows.

QUIZ

Answer these five questions. Check your answers with the answer key on page 210.

1. Item 1 of the requirements was left out in this passage. Do you remember what it was?_____

2. Is there any exception to that requirement? _____

3. Where is the section on Immigration Update?_____

4. What is one exception to the residence requirement? _____

   _____

5. Is there any exception to the requirement that you must take and understand the Oath of Allegiance to the United States?_____

   _____

If you meet the main requirements, you are ready to look at the 25 probability questions on page 64. Some of them have been asked at the naturalization hearing. These questions are asked in simple everyday English to find out how much the applicant knows about American history and government. As indicated earlier, you should know the names of your two senators and the congressman or congresswoman who represents you.

Write them here again: **SENATOR** _____

SENATOR _____

REPRESENTATIVE _____

     You have read six (6) passages containing words connected with naturalization and citizenship, and you have taken short tests on your reading. Have you done well? Do you feel that you understand the ideas expressed in the reading? Let us see about that!

     Now read number 7, the summary. See if you can explain, in your own words, about moving from alien to citizen. Practice writing about it, too.

7. Summary: How to Move from Alien to Citizen

     Moving from alien to citizen is set by law. Immigration laws are made by the Congress of the United States. Everything in this book concerning the admission of aliens, the legalization of undocumented aliens (persons not admitted as permanent residents), and the unification of families is in accord with the most recent Immigration and Nationality Act, and reflects all laws as of May 1995. A lawfully admitted alien can be naturalized if he or she meets the requirements (see page xi).

     The law states that "a person may only be naturalized as a citizen of the United States in the manner and under the conditions prescribed, and not otherwise." In this unit you have read what these conditions are. You know that what is prescribed is what must be followed. You can do it, as many before you have done!

     As one of our presidents wrote, our country is "a nation of immigrants." If the number of immigrants come in at the current rate of about 800,000 per year, we will continue this way. And some, like you, will aspire to citizenship. As you know, it takes time to become a full American citizen. Those who use their time wisely to prepare themselves will succeed.

     This is the end of Part One. Use the rest of this page to write, in your own words, an explanation of this SUMMARY!

     Then go on to Part Two. Get started now. You are on your way.

PART TWO
★★★★★★★★★★★★★★★★★★★★★★★
You Are Ready!

Climbing the Steps—An Introduction

Begin here after you pass the Pretest. You are ready! You are on your way. First, read this brief review of the law:

The Immigration and Nationality Act requires you to have an understanding of the English language, history, principles, and form of government of the United States. You must be able to read, write, and speak words in ordinary usage in the English language, UNLESS you are over 50 years old and have resided here for 20 years, or over 55 years old and have resided here for 15 years, or have a physical or developmental disability or a mental impairment. You must have a knowledge of the history, principles, and government of the United States, no matter what your age. The only exception to this requirement is a physical or mental disability. No person may apply who is opposed to our government or law, or who favors totalitarian forms of government.

Who Can Apply?

A lawfully admitted adult, 18 years or older, who has resided in the United States for five years or more as a permanent resident, or who has married a United States citizen and has lived with the spouse for three years or more.

All statements in this book are based on the Immigration and Nationality Act, and reflect regulations adopted as of May 1, 1999.

Getting Started

Read this out loud:

I am eligible for naturalization because:

- I am 18 years old or older.
- I was legally admitted for permanent residence, or I applied for legalization under the law.
- I have resided here for at least 5 years, unless I have an exemption.
- I am a person of good moral character.
- I meet the educational requirements, unless I have an exemption.

Did you understand all of that? Now read this:

This is Part Two. It contains five steps for you to follow to get ready for naturalization. They are:

Step 1: How to Begin
              Forms and Fees
              Some Questions You May Have
Step 2: Filing Your Form
              Form N-400: Now Fill Out the Real Thing
              Probability Questions
Step 3: Serious Study—English
              Practice Test of Written English
              Reading Practices I, II, and III
              Review: More Writing Practice
Step 4: Serious Study—History and Civics
              Our Government
              The Constitution
              Reading Practice
              Summary: How The Bill of Rights Protects Americans
              The Federal Government: Form and Structure
              State and Local Governments
              The Declaration of Independence
              The American Flag
              The Final Test
Step 5: The Naturalization Interview and the Oath
              Review of the Steps to Citizenship
              Review of the Probability Questions

Step 1—
How to Begin

Forms and Fees

Get the forms you need to file for naturalization. These forms may be obtained by calling the Immigration and Naturalization Service (INS) at 1-800-870-3676 (free call). You may also obtain the form from the INS page on the Internet at http://www.ins.usdoj.gov.

Having received the forms that you requested, you now should look them over carefully. Do you understand what information is needed? It may be necessary to find some of your own papers that are referred to. You should also become familiar with other forms that you may need.

If you check the Application for Naturalization, you may find that you also need other forms. The table on page 28 is a list of commonly used forms.

All fees should be paid by check or money order and should be made out to the *Immigration and Naturalization Service.*

Some of the most important of the forms listed on page 28, including the required papers that go with each, appear on the next pages. They are in the same order as the table. Also included is Biographic Information Form G-325.

Use these forms for practice even if you do not need any other than the N-400. Read the instructions carefully. Print the information, using a pen. Fill out all of the forms completely, including the personal description on the Fingerprint Card. All blanks must be filled in by printing or typing. Look for the documents you need. Look for them now. If you were ever arrested, no matter for how small an offense, look for the papers on that arrest.

FORM NUMBER	FORM TITLE	FORM FEE*
N-300	Application to File Declaration of Intention	$75
N-400	Application for Naturalization	$225
I-485	Application for Permanent Residence	$220
N-565	Application for Replacement of Naturalization or Citizenship Certificate	$135
I-90	Application to Replace Alien Registration Card	$110
I-130	Petition for Alien Relative	$110
I-817	Application for Voluntary Departure Under the Family Unity Act	$120

*As of January 1999

You Are Ready!

START HERE - Please Type or Print

Part 1. Information about you.

Family Name	Given Name	Middle Initial

Address - In care of

Street Number and Name	Apt. #

City	State or Province

Country	ZIP/Postal Code

Date of Birth (Month/Day/Year)	Country of Birth

Social Security #	A #

Part 2. Processing Information.

Date you became a permanent resident (Month/Day/Year)

Since you were admitted to the United States for Permanent Residence have you been absent for a period of six months or longer?   ☐ No   ☐ Yes - Attach a list of departure/arrival dates of all absences

Part 3. Signature. Read the information on penalties in the instructions before completing this section. You must be in the United States when you file this application. (Also sign the second page).

I desire to declare my intention to become a citizen of the United States. I certify under penalty of perjury under the laws of the United States of America that this application, and the evidence submitted with it, is all true and correct. I authorize release of any information from my records which the Immigration and Naturalization Service needs to determine eligibility for the benefit I am seeking.

Signature	Date

Part 4. Signature of person preparing form if other than above.   (sign below)

I declare that I prepared this application at the request of the above person and it is based on all information of which I have any knowledge.

Signature	Date

Print your Name

Firm Name

Firm Address

FOR INS USE ONLY

Returned	Receipt
Resubmitted	
Reloc Sent	
Reloc Rec'd	
☐ Applicant Interviewed	

Action Block

To Be Completed by Attorney or Representative, if any
☐ Fill in box if G-28 is attached to represent the applicant

VOLAG#

ATTY State License #

Form N-300 (Rev. 10/01/91)   *Continued on next page.*

Figure 4: Form N-300

Original to be retained by the Service -

Duplicate to be given to :

Family Name	Given Name	Middle Initial

Address - C/O

Street Number and Name		Apt. #
City	State or Province	
Country	ZIP/Postal Code	

Date of Birth (Month/Day/Year)	Country of Birth
Social Security #	A #

Affix

Photograph

Here

Not valid unless INS
Seal applied below

I am over the age of 18 years, have been lawfully admitted to the United States for permanent residence and am now residing in the United States pursuant to such admission.

I hereby declare my intention in good faith to become a citizen of the United States and I certify that the photographs affixed to the original and duplicate hereof are a likeness of me and were signed by me.

I do swear (affirm) that the statements I have made and the intentions I have expressed in this declaration of intention subscribed by me are true to the best of my knowledge and belief.

_____
Signature of Applicant

_____
Signature of Authorizing official

Form N-300 (Rev. 10/01/91) N

Figure 4 (cont.)

START HERE - Please Type or Print

Part 1. Information about you.

Family Name	Given Name	Middle Initial

U.S. Mailing Address - Care of

Street Number and Name		Apt. #
City	County	
State		ZIP Code
Date of Birth (month/day/year)	Country of Birth	
Social Security #	A #	

Part 2. Basis for Eligibility (check one).

a. ☐ I have been a permanent resident for at least five (5) years.

b. ☐ I have been a permanent resident for at least three (3) years and have been married to a United States Citizen for those three years.

c. ☐ I am a permanent resident child of United States citizen parent(s)

d. ☐ I am applying on the basis of qualifying military service in the Armed Forces of the U.S. and have attached completed Forms N-426 and G-325B

e. ☐ Other. (Please specify section of law)_____

Part 3. Additional information about you.

Date you became a permanent resident (month/day/year)	Port admitted with an immigrant visa or INS Office where granted adjustment of status.

Citizenship

Name on alien registration card (if different than in Part 1)

Other names used since you became a permanent resident (including maiden name)

Sex ☐ Male ☐ Female	Height	Marital Status: ☐ Single ☐ Married	☐ Divorced ☐ Widowed

Can you speak, read and write English ?   ☐No ☐Yes.

Absences from the U.S.:

Have you been absent from the U.S. since becoming a permanent resident?   ☐ No ☐Yes.

If you answered **"Yes"** , complete the following. Begin with your most recent absence. If you need more room to explain the reason for an absence or to list more trips, continue on separate paper.

Date left U.S.	Date returned	Did absence last 6 months or more?	Destination	Reason for trip
		☐ Yes ☐ No		
		☐ Yes ☐ No		
		☐ Yes ☐ No		
		☐ Yes ☐ No		
		☐ Yes ☐ No		
		☐ Yes ☐ No		

Form N-400 (Rev. 07/17/91)N   *Continued on back.*

FOR INS USE ONLY

Returned	Receipt

Resubmitted

Reloc Sent

Reloc Rec'd

☐ Applicant Interviewed

At interview

☐ request naturalization ceremony at court

Remarks

Action

To Be Completed by
***Attorney or Representative*, if any**

☐ Fill in box if G-28 is attached to represent the applicant

VOLAG#

ATTY State License #

Figure 5: Form N-400

Part 4. Information about your residences and employment.

A. List your addresses during the last five (5) years or since you became a permanent resident, whichever is less. Begin with your current address. If you need more space, continue on separate paper:

Street Number and Name, City, State, Country, and Zip Code	Dates (month/day/year)	
	From	To

B. List your employers during the last five (5) years. List your present or most recent employer first. If none, write "None". If you need more space, continue on separate paper.

Employer's Name	Employer's Address Street Name and Number - City, State and ZIP Code	Dates Employed (month/day/year)		Occupation/position
		From	To	

Part 5. Information about your marital history.

A. Total number of times you have been married _____ . If you are now married, complete the following regarding your husband or wife.

Family name	Given name	Middle initial
Address		

Date of birth (month/day/year)	Country of birth	Citizenship
Social Security#	A# (if applicable)	Immigration status (If not a U.S. citizen)

Naturalization (If applicable)
(month/day/year)   Place   (City, State)

If you have ever previously been married or if your current spouse has been previously married, please provide the following on separate paper: Name of prior spouse, date of marriage, date marriage ended, how marriage ended and immigration status of prior spouse.

Part 6. Information about your children.

B. Total Number of Children _____ Complete the following information for each of your children. If the child lives with you, state "with me" in the address column; otherwise give city/state/country of child's current residence. If deceased, write "deceased" in the address column. If you need more space, continue on separate paper.

Full name of child	Date of birth	Country of birth	Citizenship	A - Number	Address

Form N-400 (Rev 07/17/91)N

Continued on next page

Figure 5 (cont.)

Part 7. Additional eligibility factors.

Please answer each of the following questions. If your answer is **"Yes"**, explain on a separate paper.

1. Are you now, or have you ever been a member of, or in any way connected or associated with the Communist Party, or ever knowingly aided or supported the Communist Party directly, or indirectly through another organization, group or person, or ever advocated, taught, believed in, or knowingly supported or furthered the interests of communism? ☐ Yes ☐ No

2. During the period March 23, 1933 to May 8, 1945, did you serve in, or were you in any way affiliated with, either directly or indirectly, any military unit, paramilitary unit, police unit, self-defense unit, vigilante unit, citizen unit of the Nazi party or SS, government agency or office, extermination camp, concentration camp, prisoner of war camp, prison, labor camp, detention camp or transit camp, under the control or affiliated with:

    a. The Nazi Government of Germany? ☐ Yes ☐ No

    b. Any government in any area occupied by, allied with, or established with the assistance or cooperation of, the Nazi Government of Germany? ☐ Yes ☐ No

3. Have you at any time, anywhere, ever ordered, incited, assisted, or otherwise participated in the persecution of any person because of race, religion, national origin, or political opinion? ☐ Yes ☐ No

4. Have you ever left the United States to avoid being drafted into the U.S. Armed Forces? ☐ Yes ☐ No

5. Have you ever failed to comply with Selective Service laws? ☐ Yes ☐ No
    If you have registered under the Selective Service laws, complete the following information:
        Selective Service Number:_____ Date Registered:_____
    If you registered before 1978, also provide the following:
        Local Board Number:_____ Classification:_____

6. Did you ever apply for exemption from military service because of alienage, conscientious objections or other reasons? ☐ Yes ☐ No

7. Have you ever deserted from the military, air or naval forces of the United States? ☐ Yes ☐ No

8. Since becoming a permanent resident, have you ever failed to file a federal income tax return? ☐ Yes ☐ No

9. Since becoming a permanent resident, have you filed a federal income tax return as a nonresident or failed to file a federal return because you considered yourself to be a nonresident? ☐ Yes ☐ No

10 Are deportation proceedings pending against you, or have you ever been deported, or ordered deported, or have you ever applied for suspension of deportation? ☐ Yes ☐ No

11. Have you ever claimed in writing, or in any way, to be a United States citizen? ☐ Yes ☐ No

12. Have you ever:

    a. been a habitual drunkard? ☐ Yes ☐ No

    b. advocated or practiced polygamy? ☐ Yes ☐ No

    c. been a prostitute or procured anyone for prostitution? ☐ Yes ☐ No

    d. knowingly and for gain helped any alien to enter the U.S. illegally? ☐ Yes ☐ No

    e. been an illicit trafficker in narcotic drugs or marijuana? ☐ Yes ☐ No

    f. received income from illegal gambling? ☐ Yes ☐ No

    g. given false testimony for the purpose of obtaining any immigration benefit? ☐ Yes ☐ No

13. Have you ever been declared legally incompetent or have you ever been confined as a patient in a mental institution? ☐ Yes ☐ No

14. Were you born with, or have you acquired in same way, any title or order of nobility in any foreign State? ☐ Yes ☐ No

15. Have you ever:

    a. knowingly committed any crime for which you have not been arrested? ☐ Yes ☐ No

    b. been arrested, cited, charged, indicted, convicted, fined or imprisoned for breaking or violating any law or ordinance excluding traffic regulations? ☐ Yes ☐ No

(If you answer yes to 15 , in your explanation give the following information for each incident or occurrence the **city**, **state**, and **country**, where the offense took place, the **date** and **nature** of the offense, and the **outcome** or **disposition** of the case).

Part 8. Allegiance to the U.S.

If your answer to any of the following questions is **"NO"**, attach a full explanation:

    1. Do you believe in the Constitution and form of government of the U.S.? ☐ Yes ☐ No

    2. Are you willing to take the full Oath of Allegiance to the U.S.? (see instructions) ☐ Yes ☐ No

    3. If the law requires it, are you willing to bear arms on behalf of the U.S.? ☐ Yes ☐ No

    4. If the law requires it, are you willing to perform noncombatant services in the Armed Forces of the U.S.? ☐ Yes ☐ No

    5. If the law requires it, are you willing to perform work of national importance under civilian direction? ☐ Yes ☐ No

Form N-400 (Rev 07/17/91)N

Continued on back

Figure 5 (cont.)

Part 9. Memberships and organizations.

A. List your present and past membership in or affiliation with every organization, association, fund, foundation, party, club, society, or similar group in the United States or in any other place. Include any military service in this part. If none, write "none". Include the name of organization, location, dates of membership and the nature of the organization. If additional space is needed, use separate paper.

_____

_____

_____

_____

_____

Part 10. Complete only if you checked block " C " in Part 2.

How many of your parents are U.S. citizens? ☐ One ☐ Both (Give the following about one U.S. citizen parent:)

Family Name	Given Name	Middle Name

Address

Basis for citizenship:
☐ Birth
☐ Naturalization Cert. No. _____

Relationship to you (check one): ☐ natural parent ☐ adoptive parent
☐ parent of child legitimated after birth

If adopted or legitimated after birth, give date of adoption or, legitimation: *(month/day/year)* _____

Does this parent have legal custody of you? ☐ Yes ☐ No

(Attach a copy of relating evidence to establish that you are the child of this U.S. citizen and evidence of this parent's citizenship.)

Part 11. Signature. *(Read the information on penalties in the instructions before completing this section).*

I certify or, if outside the United States, I swear or affirm, under penalty of perjury under the laws of the United States of America that this application, and the evidence submitted with it, is all true and correct. I authorize the release of any information from my records which the Immigration and Naturalization Service needs to determine eligibility for the benefit I am seeking.

Signature _____ Date _____

Please Note: If you do not completely fill out this form, or fail to submit required documents listed in the instructions, you may not be found eligible for naturalization and this application may be denied.

Part 12. Signature of person preparing form if other than above. *(Sign below)*

I declare that I prepared this application at the request of the above person and it is based on all information of which I have knowledge.

Signature _____ Print Your Name _____ Date _____

Firm Name and Address

DO NOT COMPLETE THE FOLLOWING UNTIL INSTRUCTED TO DO SO AT THE INTERVIEW

I swear that I know the contents of this application, and supplemental pages 1 through _____, that the corrections, numbered 1 through _____, were made at my request, and that this amended application, is true to the best of my knowledge and belief.

Subscribed and sworn to before me by the applicant.

_____
(Examiner's Signature) Date

_____
(Complete and true signature of applicant)

Form N-400 (Rev 07/17/91)N

FPI-LOM

Figure 5 (cont.)

START HERE - Please Type or Print

Part 1. Information about you.

Family Name	Given Name	Middle Initial

Address - C/O

Street Number and Name		Apt. #

City

State	Zip Code

Date of Birth (month/day/year)	Country of Birth

Social Security #	A # (if any)

Date of Last Arrival (month/day/year)	I-94 #

Current INS Status	Expires on (month/day/year)

Part 2. Application Type. *(check one)*

I am applying for adjustment to permanent resident status because:

a. ☐ an immigrant petition giving me an immediately available immigrant visa number has been approved (attach a copy of the approval notice), or a relative, special immigrant juvenile, or special immigrant military visa petition filed with this application will give me an immediately available visa number if approved.

b. ☐ My spouse or parent applied for adjustment of status or was granted lawful permanent residence in an immigrant visa category which allows derivative status for spouses and children.

c. ☐ I entered as a K-1 fiance(e) of a U.S. citizen whom I married within 90 days of entry, or I am the K-2 child of such a fiance(e) (attach a copy of the fiance(e) petition approval notice and the marriage certificate).

d. ☐ I was granted asylum or derivative asylum status as the spouse or child of a person granted asylum and am eligible for adjustment.

e. ☐ I am a native or citizen of Cuba admitted or paroled into the U.S. after January 1, 1959, and thereafter have been physically present in the U.S. for at least 1 year.

f. ☐ I am the husband, wife, or minor unmarried child of a Cuban described in (e) and am residing with that person, and was admitted or paroled into the U.S. after January 1, 1959, and thereafter have been physically present in the U.S. for at least 1 year.

g. ☐ I have continuously resided in the U.S. since before January 1, 1972.

h. ☐ Other-explain_____

I am already a permanent resident and am applying to have the date I was granted permanent residence adjusted to the date I originally arrived in the U.S. as a nonimmigrant or parolee, or as of May 2, 1964, whichever is later, and: *(Check one)*

i. ☐ I am a native or citizen of Cuba and meet the description in (e), above.

j. ☐ I am the husband, wife or minor unmarried child of a Cuban, and meet the description in (f), above.

Form I-485 (09-09-92)N   *Continued on back.*

FOR INS USE ONLY

Returned	Receipt
_____	
_____	

Resubmitted
_____
_____

Reloc Sent
_____
_____

Reloc Rec'd
_____
_____

☐ Applicant Interviewed

Section of Law
☐ Sec. 209(b), INA
☐ Sec. 13, Act of 9/11/57
☐ Sec. 245, INA·
☐ Sec. 249, INA
☐ Sec. 1 Act of 11/2/66
☐ Sec. 2 Act of 11/2/66
☐ Other_____

Country Chargeable

Eligibility Under Sec. 245
☐ Approved Visa Petition
☐ Dependent of Principal Alien
☐ Special Immigrant
☐ Other_____

Preference

Action Block

To Be Completed by
Attorney or *Representative*, if any
☐ Fill in box if G-28 is attached to represent the applicant

VOLAG#

ATTY State License #

Figure 6: Form I-485

Part 3. Processing Information.

A. City/Town/Village of birth | Current occupation

Your mother's first name | Your father's first name

Give your name exactly how it appears on your Arrival /Departure Record (Form I-94)

Place of last entry into the U.S. (City/State) | In what status did you last enter? *(Visitor, Student, exchange alien, crewman, temporary worker, without inspection, etc.)*

Were you inspected by a U.S. Immigration Officer? ☐ Yes ☐ No

Nonimmigrant Visa Number | Consulate where Visa was issued

Date Visa was Issued (month/day/year) | Sex: ☐ Male ☐ Female | Marital Status: ☐ Married ☐ Single ☐ Divorced ☐ Widowed

Have you ever before applied for permanent resident status in the U.S? ☐ No ☐ Yes (give date and place of filing and final disposition):

B. List your present husband/wife, all of your sons and daughters (if you have none, write "none". If additional space is needed, use separate paper).

Family Name	Given Name	Middle Initial	Date of Birth (month/day/year)
Country of birth	Relationship	A #	Applying with you? ☐ Yes ☐ No
Family Name	Given Name	Middle Initial	Date of Birth (month/day/year)
Country of birth	Relationship	A #	Applying with you? ☐ Yes ☐ No
Family Name	Given Name	Middle Initial	Date of Birth (month/day/year)
Country of birth	Relationship	A #	Applying with you? ☐ Yes ☐ No
Family Name	Given Name	Middle Initial	Date of Birth (month/day/year)
Country of birth	Relationship	A #	Applying with you? ☐ Yes ☐ No
Family Name	Given Name	Middle Initial	Date of Birth (month/day/year)
Country of birth	Relationship	A #	Applying with you? ☐ Yes ☐ No

C. List your present and past membership in or affiliation with every political organization, association, fund, foundation, party, club, society, or similar group in the United States or in any other place since your 16th birthday. Include any foreign military service in this part. If none, write "none". Include the name of organization, location, dates of membership from and to, and the nature of the organization. If additional space is needed, use separate paper.

_____
_____
_____
_____
_____
_____
_____

Form I-485 (Rev. 09-09-92) N   Continued On Next Page

Figure 6: (cont.)

Part 3. Processing Information. *(Continued)*

Please answer the following questions. (If your answer is **"Yes"** on any one of these questions, explain on a separate piece of paper. Answering **"Yes"** does not necessarily mean that you are not entitled to register for permanent residence or adjust status).

1. Have you ever, in or outside the U. S.:
   a. knowingly committed any crime of moral turpitude or a drug-related offense for which you have not been arrested?
   b. been arrested, cited, charged, indicted, fined, or imprisoned for breaking or violating any law or ordinance, excluding traffic violations?
   c. been the beneficiary of a pardon, amnesty, rehabilitation decree, other act of clemency or similar action?
   d. exercised diplomatic immunity to avoid prosecution for a criminal offense in the U. S.? ☐ Yes ☐ No

2. Have you received public assistance in the U.S. from any source, including the U.S. government or any state, county, city, or municipality (other than emergency medical treatment) , or are you likely to receive public assistance in the future? ☐ Yes ☐ No

3. Have you ever:
   a. within the past 10 years been a prostitute or procured anyone for prostitution, or intend to engage in such activities in the future?
   b. engaged in any unlawful commercialized vice, including, but not limited to, illegal gambling?
   c. knowingly encouraged, induced, assisted, abetted or aided any alien to try to enter the U.S. illegally?
   d. illicitly trafficked in any controlled substance, or knowingly assisted, abetted or colluded in the illicit trafficking of any controlled substance? ☐ Yes ☐ No

4. Have you ever engaged in, conspired to engage in, or do you intend to engage in, or have you ever solicited membership or funds for, or have you through any means ever assisted or provided any type of material support to, any person or organization that has ever engaged or conspired to engage, in sabotage, kidnapping, political assassination, hijacking, or any other form of terrorist activity? ☐ Yes ☐ No

5. Do you intend to engage in the U.S. in:
   a. espionage?
   b. any activity a purpose of which is opposition to, or the control or overthrow of, the Government of the United States, by force, violence or other unlawful means?
   c. any activity to violate or evade any law prohibiting the export from the United States of goods, technology or sensitive information? ☐ Yes ☐ No

6. Have you ever been a member of, or in any way affiliated with, the Communist Party or any other totalitarian party? ☐ Yes ☐ No

7. Did you, during the period March 23, 1933 to May 8, 1945, in association with either the Nazi Government of Germany or any organization or government associated or allied with the Nazi Government of Germany, ever order, incite, assist or otherwise participate in the persecution of any person because of race, religion, national origin or political opinion? ☐ Yes ☐ No

8. Have you ever engaged in genocide, or otherwise ordered, incited, assisted or otherwise participated in the killing of any person because of race, religion, nationality, ethnic origin, or political opinion? ☐ Yes ☐ No

9. Have you ever been deported from the U.S., or removed from the U.S. at government expense, excluded within the past year, or are you now in exclusion or deportation proceedings? ☐ Yes ☐ No

10. Are you under a final order of civil penalty for violating section 274C of the Immigration Act for use of fraudulent documents, or have you, by fraud or willful misrepresentation of a material fact, ever sought to procure, or procured, a visa, other documentation, entry into the U.S., or any other immigration benefit? ☐ Yes ☐ No

11. Have you ever left the U.S. to avoid being drafted into the U.S. Armed Forces? ☐ Yes ☐ No

12. Have you ever been a J nonimmigrant exchange visitor who was subject to the 2 year foreign residence requirement and not yet complied with that requirement or obtained a waiver? ☐ Yes ☐ No

13. Are you now withholding custody of a U.S. Citizen child outside the U.S. from a person granted custody of the child? ☐ Yes ☐ No

14. Do you plan to practice polygamy in the U.S.? ☐ Yes ☐ No

Continued on back

Figure 6: (cont.)

Part 4. Signature. *(Read the information on penalties in the instructions before completing this section. You must file this application while in the United States.)*

I certify under penalty of perjury under the laws of the United States of America that this application, and the evidence submitted with it, is all true and correct. I authorize the release of any information from my records which the Immigration and Naturalization Service needs to determine eligibility for the benefit I am seeking.

Signature	Print Your Name	Date	Daytime Phone Number

Please Note: *If you do not completely fill out this form, or fail to submit required documents listed in the instructions, you may not be found eligible for the requested document and this application may be denied.*

Part 5. Signature of person preparing form if other than above. *(Sign Below)*

I declare that I prepared this application at the request of the above person and it is based on all information of which I have knowledge.

Signature	Print Your Name	Date	Day time Phone Number

Firm Name
and Address

FPI-LOM

Figure 6: (cont.)

START HERE - Please Type or Print

FOR INS USE ONLY

Part 1. Information about Applicant

Family Name	First Name	Middle Name

Address - C/O

Street Number and Name		Apt. Suite
City	State or Province	
Country		ZIP/Postal Code

INS A #	Date of Birth *(month/day/year)*	Country of Birth

Part 2. Basis for Eligibility *(check one)*

1. On Form I-485, Part 2, I checked application type *(check one):*

a. ☐ An immigrant petition . . .   Go to #2.
b. ☐ My spouse or parent applied . . .   Go to #2.
c. ☐ I entered as a K-1 fiance . . .   Stop Here. Do Not File This Form.
d. ☐ I was granted asylum . . .   Stop Here. Do Not File This Form.
e. ☐ I am a native or citizen of Cuba . .   Stop Here. Do Not File This Form.
f. ☐ I am the spouse or child of a Cuban   Stop Here. Do Not File This Form.
g. ☐ I have continuously resided in the U.S. . Stop Here. Do Not File This Form.
h. ☐ Other . . .   Go to #2.
i. ☐ I am already a permanent resident . . .   Stop Here. Do Not File This Form.
j. ☐ I am already a permanent resident and   Stop Here. Do Not File This Form.
   am the spouse or child of a Cuban

2. I have filed Form I-360; and I am applying for adjustment of status as a special immigrant juvenile court dependent *(check one):*

   ☐ Yes Stop Here. Do Not File This Form.   ☐ No Go to #3.

3. I have filed Form I-360; and I am applying for adjustment of status as a special immigrant who has served in the United States Armed Forces *(check one):*
   ☐ Yes Stop Here. Do Not File This Form.   ☐ No Go to #4.

4. I last entered the United States *(check one):*

   ☐ Legally as a crewman (D-1/D-2 visa). Go to #11.   ☐ Legally without a visa   Go to #5.
   ☐ Without inspection.   Go to #11.   ☐ Legally as a parolee.   Go to #5.
   ☐ Legally in transit without visa status. Go to #11.   ☐ Legally with another type of visa (show type _____) Go to #5.

5. I last entered the United States legally without a visa as a visitor for tourism or business; and I am applying for adjustment of status as the spouse, unmarried child less than 21 years old, parent, widow or widower of a United States citizen *(check one):*

   ☐ Yes Stop Here. Do Not File This Form.   ☐ No Go to #6.

6. I last entered the United States legally as a parolee, or with a visa (except as a crewman), or as a Canadian citizen without a visa; and I am applying for adjustment of status *(check one):*

   ☐ As the spouse, unmarried child less than 21 years old, parent, widow or widower of a United States citizen.
   Stop Here. Do Not File This Form.

   ☐ As a special immigrant retired international organization employee or family member of an international organization employee or as a special immigrant physician; and I have filed Form I-360. Stop Here. Do Not File This Form.

   ☐ Under some other category. Go to #7.

FOR INS USE ONLY column:

Returned
_____
_____

Resubmitted
_____
_____

Reloc Sent
_____
_____

Reloc Rec'd
_____
_____

Receipt

Interviewed
☐
☐

File Reviewed   Class of Adjustment Code:
☐
☐   ___ ___ ___

To Be Completed by Attorney or Representative, if any

☐ Check if G-28 is attached showing you represent the petitioner

VOLAG#

ATTY State License #

Figure 7: Form I-485 Supplement A

39

7. I am a national of the (former) Soviet Union, Vietnam, Laos or Cambodia who last entered the United States legally as a public interest parolee after having been denied refugee status; and I am applying for adjustment of status under Public Law 101-167 *(check one)*:

   ☐ Yes **Stop Here. Do Not File This Form.**   ☐ No **Go to #8.**

8. I have been employed in the United States after 01/01/77 without INS authorization *(check one)*:

   ☐ Yes **Go to #9.**   ☐ No **Go to #10.**

9. I am applying for adjustment of status under the Immigration Nursing Relief Act (INRA); I was employed without INS authorization only on or before 11/29/90; and I have always maintained a lawful immigration status while in the United States after 11/05/86 *(check one)*:

   ☐ Yes **Stop Here. Do Not File This Form.**   ☐ No **Go to #10.**

10. I am now in lawful immigration status; and I have always maintained a lawful immigration status while in the United States after 11/05/86 *(check one)*:

    ☐ Yes **Stop Here. Do Not File This Form .**
    ☐ No, but I believe that INS will determine that my failure to be in or maintain a lawful immigration status was through no fault of my own or for technical reasons. **Stop Here. Do Not File This Form,** and attach an explanation to your Form I-485 application.
    ☐ No **Go to #11.**

11. I am unmarried and less than 17 years old *(check one)*:

    ☐ Yes **Stop Here. File This Form and Form I-485.**   Pay only the fee required with Form I-485.
    ☐ No **Go to #12.**

12. I am the unmarried child of a legalized alien and am less than 21 years old, or I am the spouse of a legalized alien; and I have attached a copy of my receipt or approval notice showing that I have properly filed Form I-817, Application for Voluntary Departure under the Family Unity Program *(check one)*:

    ☐ Yes **Stop Here. File This Form and Form I-485.**   Pay only the fee required with Form I-485.
    ☐ No **Go to #13.**

13. **File This Form and Form I-485. You must pay the additional sum:**

    > $130.00 - Fee required with Form I-485* <u>and</u>
    > $650.00 - Additional sum under section 245(i) of the Act
    > ————
    > **$780.00** - Total amount you must pay.

*If you filed Form I-485 separately, attach a copy of your filing receipt and pay only the additional sum of $650.00. In # 11 and /or # 12, show the answer you would have given on the date you filed Form I-485.

Part 3.   Signature. Read the information on penalties in the instructions before completing this section. If someone helped you prepare this petition he or she must complete Part 4.

I certify, under penalty of perjury under the laws of the United States of America, that this application, and the evidence submitted with it, is all true and correct. I authorize the release of any information from my records which the Immigration and Naturalization Service needs to determine eligibility for the benefit I am seeking.

Signature	Print Your Name	Date	Daytime Telephone No.

Please Note: If you do not completely fill out this form or fail to submit required documents listed in the instructions, you may not be found eligible for the requested document and this application may be denied.

Part 4.   Signature of person preparing form if other than above. *(Sign Below)*

I declare that I prepared this application at the request of the above person and it is based on all information of which I have knowledge.

Signature	Print Your Name	Date	Daytime Telephone No.

Firm Name
and Address

Form I-485 (09/30/94) Supplement A

Form 9003
(January 1992)

Additional Questions to be Completed by All Applicants
for Permanent Residence in the United States

OMB Clearance No. 1545-1065
Expires 8-31-94

This form must accompany your application for permanent residence in the United States

Privacy Act Notice: Your responses to the following questions will be provided to the Internal Revenue Service pursuant to Section 6039E of the Internal Revenue Code of 1986. Use of this information is limited to that needed for tax administration purposes. Failure to provide this information may result in a $500 penalty unless failure is due to reasonable cause.

On the date of issuance of the Alien Registration Receipt Card, the Immigration and Naturalization Service will send the following information to the Internal Revenue Service: your name, social security number, address, date of birth, alien identification number, occupation, class of admission, and answers to IRS Form 9003.

Name *(Last—Surname—Family)*   *(First—Given)*   *(Middle Initial)*

Taxpayer Identification Number . . . .

Enter your Social Security Number (SSN) if you have one. If you do not
have an SSN but have used a Taxpayer Identification Number issued to you
by the Internal Revenue Service, enter that number. Otherwise, write "NONE"
in the space provided; i.e., " ⌐ ⌐ ⌐ ⌐ |N,O,N,E, ".

	Mark appropriate column	
	Yes	No
1. Are you self-employed? Mark "yes" if you own and actively operate a business in which you share in the profits other than as an investor.		
2. Have you been in the United States for 183 days or more during any one of the three calendar years immediately preceding the current calendar year? Mark "yes" if you spent 183 days or more (not necessarily consecutive) in the United States during any **one of the three prior** calendar years **whether or not you worked** in the United States.		
3. During the last three years did you receive income from sources in the United States? Mark "yes" if you received income paid by individuals or institutions located in the United States. Income includes, but is not limited to, compensation for services provided by you, interest, dividends, rents, and royalties.		
4. Did you file a United States Individual Income Tax Return (Forms 1040, 1040A, 1040EZ or 1040NR) in any of the last three years?		

If you answered yes to question 4, for which tax year was the last return filed? . . . . 19 __ __

Paperwork Reduction Act Notice—We ask for the information on this form to carry out the Internal Revenue laws of the United States. You are required to give us the information. We need it to ensure that you are complying with these laws and to allow us to figure and collect the right amount of tax.

The time needed to complete and file this form will vary depending on individual circumstances. The estimated average time is 5 minutes. If you have comments concerning the accuracy of this time estimate or suggestions for making this form more simple, we would be happy to hear from you. You can write to both the **Internal Revenue Service,** Washington, DC 20224. Attention: IRS Reports Clearance Officer, T:FP, and **Office of Management and Budget.** Paperwork Reduction Project (1545-1065) Washington, DC 20503. **DO NOT send this form to either of these offices. Instead, return it to the appropriate office of the Department of State or the Immigration and Naturalization Service.**

Remarks

Cat. No. 10126D

2. FOR ADIT AND STATISTICAL REPORTS

Form **9003** (Rev. 1-92)

Figure 8: Form 9003

FORM G-325A
BIOGRAPHIC INFORMATION

OMB No. 1115-0066

(Family name)	(First name)	(Middle name)	☐ MALE ☐ FEMALE	BIRTHDATE (Mo.-Day-Yr.)	NATIONALITY	FILE NUMBER A-

ALL OTHER NAMES USED (Including names by previous marriages)	CITY AND COUNTRY OF BIRTH	SOCIAL SECURITY NO. (If any)

	FAMILY NAME	FIRST NAME	DATE, CITY AND COUNTRY OF BIRTH (If known)	CITY AND COUNTRY OF RESIDENCE
FATHER				
MOTHER (Maiden name)				

HUSBAND (If none, so state) OR WIFE	FAMILY NAME (For wife, give maiden name)	FIRST NAME	BIRTHDATE	CITY & COUNTRY OF BIRTH	DATE OF MARRIAGE	PLACE OF MARRIAGE

FORMER HUSBANDS OR WIVES (if none, so state)

FAMILY NAME (For wife, give maiden name)	FIRST NAME	BIRTHDATE	DATE & PLACE OF MARRIAGE	DATE AND PLACE OF TERMINATION OF MARRIAGE

APPLICANT'S RESIDENCE LAST FIVE YEARS. LIST PRESENT ADDRESS FIRST.

STREET AND NUMBER	CITY	PROVINCE OR STATE	COUNTRY	FROM MONTH	FROM YEAR	TO MONTH	TO YEAR
						PRESENT TIME	

APPLICANT'S LAST ADDRESS OUTSIDE THE UNITED STATES OF MORE THAN ONE YEAR

STREET AND NUMBER	CITY	PROVINCE OR STATE	COUNTRY	FROM MONTH	FROM YEAR	TO MONTH	TO YEAR

APPLICANT'S EMPLOYMENT LAST FIVE YEARS. (IF NONE, SO STATE.) LIST PRESENT EMPLOYMENT FIRST

FULL NAME AND ADDRESS OF EMPLOYER	OCCUPATION (SPECIFY)	FROM MONTH	FROM YEAR	TO MONTH	TO YEAR
				PRESENT TIME	

Show below last occupation abroad if not shown above. (Include all information requested above.)

THIS FORM IS SUBMITTED IN CONNECTION WITH APPLICATION FOR: ☐ NATURALIZATION ☐ STATUS AS PERMANENT RESIDENT ☐ OTHER (SPECIFY):	SIGNATURE OF APPLICANT	DATE

Are all copies legible? ☐ Yes	IF YOUR NATIVE ALPHABET IS IN OTHER THAN ROMAN LETTERS, WRITE YOUR NAME IN YOUR NATIVE ALPHABET IN THIS SPACE:

PENALTIES: SEVERE PENALTIES ARE PROVIDED BY LAW FOR KNOWINGLY AND WILLFULLY FALSIFYING OR CONCEALING A MATERIAL FACT.

APPLICANT: BE SURE TO PUT YOUR NAME AND ALIEN REGISTRATION NUMBER IN THE BOX OUTLINED BY HEAVY BORDER BELOW.

COMPLETE THIS BOX (Family name)	(Given name)	(Middle name)	(Alien registration number)

Form G-325 A (Rev. 10-1-82)   (1) Ident.

Figure 9: Form G-325A

OMB #1115-0015

U.S. Department of Justice
Immigration and Naturalization Service

Application for Replacement
Naturalization/Citizenship Document

START HERE - Please Type or Print

Part 1. Information about you.

Family Name	Given Name	Middle Name

Address - In care of:

Street # and Name		Apt #

City or town	State or Province

Country	Zip or Postal Code

Date of Birth *(Month/Day/Year)*	Country of Birth

Certificate #	A #

Part 2. Type of application.

1. I hereby apply for: (check one)

a. ☐ a new Certificate of Citizenship

b. ☐ a new Certificate of Naturalization

c. ☐ a new Certificate of Repatriation

d. ☐ a new Declaration of Intention

e. ☐ a special Certificate of Naturalization to obtain recognition of my U.S. citizenship by a foreign country

2. Basis for application: (If you checked other than "e" in Part 1, check one)

a. ☐ my certificate is/was lost, stolen or destroyed (attach a copy of the certificate if you have one). Explain when, where and how _____

_____
_____

b. ☐ my certificate is mutilated (attach the certificate)

c. ☐ my name has been changed (attach the certificate)

d. ☐ my certificate or declaration is incorrect (attach the documents)

Part 3. Processing Information.

SEX ☐ Male ☐ Female	Height	Marital Status ☐ Single ☐ Married	☐ Widowed ☐ Divorced

My last certificate or declaration of intention was issued to me by:

INS Office or Name of court	Date *(Month/Day/Year)*

Name in which the document was issued:
_____

Other names I have used (if none, so indicate):
_____

Since becoming a citizen, have you lost your citizenship in any manner?

☐ No   ☐ Yes (attach an explanation)

Part 4. Complete if applying for a new document because of name change.

Name changed to present name by: (check one)

☐ Marriage or Divorce on (month/day/year)_____(attach a copy of marriage or divorce certificate)

☐ Court Decree (month/day/year)_____(attach a copy of the court decree)

Form N-565 (Rev. 11/18/93) N   ***Continued on back.***

FOR INS USE ONLY

Returned	Receipt

Resubmitted	

Reloc Sent	

Reloc Rec'd	

☐ Applicant Interviewed

☐ Declaration of Intention verified by
_____

☐ Citizenship verified by
_____

Remarks

Action Block

To Be Completed by
Attorney or Representative, if any

☐ Fill in box if G-28 is attached to represent the applicant

VOLAG#

ATTY State License #

Figure 10: Form N-565

Part 5.   Complete if applying to correct your document.

If you are applying for a new certificate or declaration of intention because your current one is incorrect, explain why it is incorrect and attach copies of the documents supporting your request.

_____

_____

_____

_____

Part 6.   Complete if applying for a special certificate of recognition as a citizen of the U.S. by the Government of the foreign country.

Name of Foreign Country_____

Information about official of the country who has requested this certificate (if known)

Name   Official title

_____

Government Agency

_____

Address: Street # and Name		Room #
City	State or Province	
Country		Zip or Postal Code

Part 7.   Signature. *Read the information on penalties in the instructions before completing this part. If you are going to file this application at an INS office in the U.S., sign below.   If you are going to file it at a U.S. INS office overseas, sign in front of a U.S. INS or consular official.*

I certify, or, if outside the United States, I swear or affirm, under penalty of perjury under the laws of the United States of America that this application, and the evidence submitted with it, is all true and correct. I authorize the release of any information from my records which the Immigration and Naturalization Service needs to determine eligibility for the benefit I am seeking.

Signature	Date

Signature of INS or Consular Official	Print Name	Date

Please Note: *If you do not completely fill out this form, or fail to submit required documents listed in the instructions, you may not be found eligible for a certificate and this application may be denied.*

Part 8.   Signature of person preparing form if other than above.   (sign below)

I declare that I prepared this application at the request of the above person and it is based on all information of which I have knowledge.

Signature	Print Your Name	Date

Firm Name
and Address

☆ U.S. GPO:1994-301-164/92718

Form N-565 (Rev. 11/18/93)N

Figure 10: (cont.)

START HERE - Please Type or Print

Part 1. Information about you.

Family Name	Given Name	Middle Initial

U.S. Mailing Address - C/O

Street Number and Name	Apt. #
City	

State	ZIP Code

Date of Birth (Month/Day/Year)	Country of Birth

Social Security #	A #

Part 2. Application Type.

1. My status is: (check one)

- a. ☐ Permanent Resident
- b. ☐ Conditional Resident

2. Reason for application: (check one)

I am a permanent resident or conditional resident and:

- a. ☐ my card was lost, stolen, or destroyed. I have attached a copy of an *identity document*
- b. ☐ I never received a card. I have attached a copy of an *identity document*
- c. ☐ my card is mutilated. I have attached the mutilated card.
- d. ☐ my card was incorrect when issued. I have attached the incorrect card and evidence of the correct information.
- e. ☐ my name or other Biographic information has changed since the card was issued. I have attached my present card and evidence of the new information.

I am a permanent resident and :

- f. ☐ my present card is expiring. I have attached my present card.
- g. ☐ I have reached my 14th birthday. I have attached my present card and a Fingerprint Card (Form FD-258)
- h. ☐ I was a commuter and am now taking up residence in the U.S. I have attached my present card and evidence of my residence in the U.S.
- i. ☐ my status has been automatically converted to permanent resident. I have attached my Temporary Status Document.
- j ☐ I have an old edition of the card. My present card is attached.

Part 3. Processing Information.

Mother's First Name	Father's First Name
City of Residence where you applied for an Immigrant Visa or Adjustment of Status	Consulate where Immigrant Visa was issued or INS office where status was Adjusted
City/Town/Village of Birth	Date of Admission as an immigrant or Adjustment of Status

Form I-90 (Rev. 10/01/91) N

Continued on back.

FOR INS USE ONLY

Returned	Receipt

Resubmitted	

Reloc Sent	

Reloc Rec'd	

☐ Applicant Interviewed

Status as _____ verfied by _____
         Class   Inititals

FD-258 forwarded on _____
I-89 Forwarded on _____

Remarks

Action Block

To Be Completed by
***Attorney* or *Representative*, if any**

☐ Fill in box if G-28 is attached to represent the applicant

VOLAG#

ATTY State License #

Figure 11: (cont.)

Part 3. Processing Information (con't):

If you entered the U.S. with an Immigrant Visa, also complete the following:

Destination in U.S. at time
of Admission

Port of Entry where Admitted
to U.S.

Are you in deportation or exclusion proceedings?　　□ No　　□ Yes

Since you were granted permanent residence, have you ever filed Form I-407, Abandonment by Alien of Status as Lawful Permanent Resident, or otherwise been judged to have abandoned your status?　　□ No　　□ Yes
If you answer "yes" to any of the above questions , explain in detail on a separate piece of paper

Part 4.　　Signature. *(Read the information on penalties in the instructions before completing this section. You must file this application while in the United States.)*

I certify under penalty of perjury under the laws of the United States of America that this application, and the evidence submitted with it, is all true and correct. I authorize the release of any information from my records which the Immigration and Naturalization Service needs to determine eligibility for the benefit I am seeking.

Signature　　　　　　　　　　　　　　　　　　*Date*　　　　　*Daytime Phone Number*

Please Note: If you do not completely fill out this form, or fail to submit required documents listed in the instructions, you cannot be found eligible for the requested document and this application may to be denied.

Part 5.　　Signature of person preparing form if other than above. *(Sign below)*

I declare that I prepared this application at the request of the above person and it is based on all information of which I have knowledge.

Signature　　　　　**Print Your Name**　　　　　**Date**　　　*Daytime Phone Number*

Firm Name
and Address

For sale by the U.S. Government Printing Office
Superintendent of Documents, Mail Stop: SSOP, Washington, DC 20402-9328
★U.S. GPO: 1991-312-328/51125

Form I-90 (Rev. 10/0191) N

Figure 11: Form I-90

DO NOT WRITE IN THIS BLOCK - FOR EXAMINING OFFICE ONLY

Case ID#	Action Stamp	Fee Stamp

A#

G-28 or Volag #

Section of Law:
- [ ] 201 (b) spouse
- [ ] 201 (b) child
- [ ] 201 (b) parent
- [ ] 203 (a)(1)
- [ ] 203 (a)(2)
- [ ] 203 (a)(4)
- [ ] 203 (a)(5)

AM CON: _____

Petition was filed on: _____ (priority date)
- [ ] Personal Interview
- [ ] Pet. [ ] Ben. "A" File Reviewed
- [ ] Field Investigations
- [ ] 204 (a)(2)(A) Resolved
- [ ] Previously Forwarded
- [ ] Stateside Criteria
- [ ] I-485 Simultaneously
- [ ] 204 (h) Resolved

Remarks:

A. Relationship

1. **The alien relative is my**
   - [ ] Husband/Wife
   - [ ] Parent
   - [ ] Brother/Sister
   - [ ] Child

2. Are you related by adoption?
   - [ ] Yes
   - [ ] No

3. Did you gain permanent residence through adoption?
   - [ ] Yes
   - [ ] No

B. Information about you

1. **Name** (Family name in CAPS) (First) (Middle)

2. **Address** (Number and Street) (Apartment Number)

   (Town or City) (State/Country) (ZIP/Postal Code)

3. **Place of Birth** (Town or City) (State/Country)

4. **Date of Birth** (Mo/Day/Yr)
5. **Sex** [ ] Male [ ] Female
6. **Marital Status** [ ] Married [ ] Single [ ] Widowed [ ] Divorced

7. **Other Names Used** (including maiden name)

8. **Date and Place of Present Marriage** (if married)

9. **Social Security Number**
10. **Alien Registration Number** (if any)

11. **Names of Prior Husbands/Wives**
12. **Date(s) Marriages(s) Ended**

13. **If you are a U.S. citizen, complete the following:**
    My citizenship was acquired through (check one)
    - [ ] Birth in the U.S.
    - [ ] Naturalization (Give number of certificate, date and place it was issued)
    - [ ] Parents
      Have you obtained a certificate of citizenship in your own name?
      - [ ] Yes
      - [ ] No
      If "Yes", give number of certificate, date and place it was issued

14a. **If you are a lawful permanent resident alien, complete the following:**
     Date and place of admission for, or adjustment to, lawful permanent residence, and class of admission:

14b. **Did you gain permanent resident status through marriage to a United States citizen or lawful permanent resident?** [ ] Yes [ ] No

C. Information about your alien relative

1. **Name** (Family name in CAPS) (First) (Middle)

2. **Address** (Number and Street) (Apartment Number)

   (Town or City) (State/Country) (ZIP/Postal Code)

3. **Place of Birth** (Town or City) (State/Country)

4. **Date of Birth** (Mo/Day/Yr)
5. **Sex** [ ] Male [ ] Female
6. **Marital Status** [ ] Married [ ] Single [ ] Widowed [ ] Divorced

7. **Other Names Used** (including maiden name)

8. **Date and Place of Present Marriage** (if married)

9. **Social Security Number**
10. **Alien Registration Number** (if any)

11. **Names of Prior Husbands/Wives**
12. **Date(s) Marriages(s) Ended**

13. **Has your relative ever been in the U.S.?**
    - [ ] Yes
    - [ ] No

14. **If your relative is currently in the U.S., complete the following:** He or she last arrived as a (visitor, student, stowaway, without inspection, etc.)

    Arrival/Departure Record (I-94) Number   Date arrived (Month/Day/Year)

    Date authorized stay expired, or will expire, as shown on Form I-94 or I-95

15. **Name and address of present employer** (if any)

    Date this employment began (Month/Day/Year)

16. **Has you relative ever been under immigration proceedings?**
    - [ ] Yes
    - [ ] No Where _____ When _____
    - [ ] Exclusion
    - [ ] Deportation
    - [ ] Recission
    - [ ] Judicial Proceedings

INITIAL RECEIPT	RESUBMITTED	RELOCATED		COMPLETED		
		Rec'd	Sent	Approved	Denied	Returned

Form I-130 (Rev. 4/11/91) Y

Figure 12: Form I-130

C. (continued) Information about your alien relative

16. List husband/wife and all children of your relative (if your relative is your husband/wife, list only his or her children).

(Name)	(Relationship)	(Date of Birth)	(Country of Birth)

17. Address in the United States where your relative intends to live

(Number and Street)   (Town or City)   (State)

18. Your relative's address abroad

(Number and Street)   (Town or City)   (Province)   (Country)   (Phone Number)

19. If your relative's native alphabet is other than Roman letters, write his or her name and address abroad in the native alphabet:

(Name)   (Number and Street)   (Town or City)   (Province)   (Country)

20. If filing for your husband/wife, give last address at which you both lived together:

(Name)   (Number and Street)   (Town or City)   (Province)   (Country)   **From** (Month) (Year)   **To** (Month) (Year)

21. Check the appropriate box below and give the information required for the box you checked:

☐ Your relative will apply for a visa abroad at the American Consulate in _____
                                                            (City)   (Country)

☐ Your relative is in the United States and will apply for adjustment of status to that of a lawful permanent resident in the office of the Immigration and Naturalization Service at _____. If your relative is not eligible for adjustment of status, he or she will
                                  (City)   (State)

apply for a visa abroad at the American Consulate in _____
                                    (City)   (Country)

(Designation of a consulate outside the country of your relative's last residence does not guarantee acceptance for processing by that consulate. Acceptance is at the discretion of the designated consulate.)

D. Other Information

1. If separate petitions are also being submitted for other relatives, give names of each and relationship.

2. Have you ever filed a petition for this or any other alien before?   ☐ Yes   ☐ No
If "Yes," give name, place and date of filing, and result.

Warning: The INS investigates claimed relationships and verifies the validity of documents. The INS seeks criminal prosecutions when family relationships are falsified to obtain visas.

Penalties: You may, by law be imprisoned for not more than five years, or fined $250,000, or both, for entering into a marriage contract for the purpose of evading any provision of the immigration laws and you may be fined up to $10,000 or imprisoned up to five years or both, for knowingly and willfully falsifying or concealing a material fact or using any false document in submitting this petition.

Your Certification: I certify, under penalty of perjury under the laws of the United States of America, that the foregoing is true and correct. Furthermore, I authorize the release of any information from my records which the Immigration and Naturalization Service needs to determine eligibility for the benefit that I am seeking.

Signature _____ Date _____ Phone Number _____

Signature of Person Preparing Form if Other than Above

I declare that I prepared this document at the request of the person above and that it is based on all information of which I have any knowledge.

Print Name _____ (Address) _____ (Signature) _____ (Date) _____

G-28 ID Number _____

Volag Number _____

Figure 12: (cont.)

NOTICE TO PERSONS FILING FOR SPOUSES IF MARRIED LESS THAN TWO YEARS

Pursuant to section 216 of the Immigration and Nationality Act, your alien spouse may be granted conditional permanent resident status in the United States as of the date he or she is admitted or adjusted to conditional status by an officer of the Immigration and Naturalization Service. Both you and your conditional permanent resident spouse are required to file a petition, Form I-751, Joint Petition to Remove Conditional Basis of Alien's Permanent Resident Status, during the ninety day period immediately before the second anniversary of the date your alien spouse was granted conditional permanent residence.

Otherwise, the rights, privileges, responsibilities and duties which apply to all other permanent residents apply equally to a conditional permanent resident. A conditional permanent resident is not limited to the right to apply for naturalization, to file petitions in behalf of qualifying relatives, or to reside permanently in the United States as an immigrant in accordance with the immigration laws.

> **Failure to file Form I-751, Joint Petition to Remove the Conditional Basis of Alien's Permanent Resident Status, will result in termination of permanent residence status and initiation of deportation proceedings.**

NOTE: You must complete Items 1 through 6 to assure that petition approval is recorded. Do not write in the section below item 6.

1. **Name of relative** (Family name in CAPS)   (First)   (Middle)

2. **Other names used by relative** (Including maiden name)

3. **Country of relative's birth**   4. **Date of relative's birth** (Month/Day/Year)

5. **Your name** (Last name in CAPS) (First)   (Middle)   6. **Your phone number**

Action Stamp

SECTION	DATE PETITION FILED
☐ 201 (b)(spouse)	
☐ 201 (b)(child)	
☐ 201 (b)(parent)	
☐ 203 (a)(1)	☐ STATESIDE
☐ 203 (a)(2)	CRITERIA GRANTED
☐ 203 (a)(4)	
☐ 203 (a)(5)	SENT TO CONSUL AT;

Relative Petition Card
Form I-130A (Rev. 4/11/91) Y

CHECKLIST

Have you answered each question?
Have you signed the petition?
Have you enclosed:

☐ The filing fee for each petition?
☐ Proof of your citizenship or lawful permanent residence?
☐ All required supporting documents for each petition?

If you are filing for your husband or wife have you included:

☐ Your picture?
☐ His or her picture?
☐ Your G-325A?
☐ His or her G-325A?

Figure 12: (cont.)

49

START HERE - Please Type or Print

PART 1. Information about you, the applicant for Family Unity Benefits

Family Name	Given Name	Middle Initial

Address - C/O

Street		Apt. #
City	State	Zip Code

Date of Birth (month/day/year)	Country of Birth
Social Security # *(If any)*	A# *(If any)*
Date of Arrival month/day/year	I-94# *(If any)*
Current Immigration Status	Expires on (month/day/year)

Part 2. Type of Application.

1. Relationship to a legalized alien *(check one):*

   a. ☐ I am the spouse of a legalized alien and have been married to him or her since at least May 5, 1988.

   b. ☐ I am the unmarried child of a legalized alien and this relationship was established before May 5, 1988.

2. I am applying for *(check one):*

   a. ☐ Initial voluntary departure under the Family Unity Program.

   b. ☐ An extension of voluntary departure granted under the Family Unity Program.

Part 3. Information about the legalized alien you are related to.

Family Name	Given Name	Middle Initial

Address - C/O

Street Number and Name		Apt. #
City	State	Zip Code

Date of Birth (month/day/year)	Country of Birth
Social Security #	A#

Part 4. Processing Information.

A. If separate applications for Family Unity benefits are also being submitted for other relatives, give names of each and list relationship. _____

B. Have you ever applied for Family Unity benefits before?   ☐ Yes   ☐ No

C. If "Yes", give name under which you applied, place and date of filing, #A assigned, and result.

   _____
   _____

Form I-817 (Rev. 09/10/91)N   *Continued on back.*

Figure 13: Form I-817

Part 4. Processing Information (con't).

D. Have you ever been in exclusion or deportation proceedings? ☐ No ☐ Yes. If yes, explain on a separate sheet, including where and when the proceedings took place.

E. Address where you resided in the United States on May 5, 1988

Street	Apt. #	City	State	Zip Code

F. Answer the following. If your answer is **yes** to any question, explain in detail on a separate sheet.

1. Have you ever, in or outside the U. S.:
   a. knowingly committed a crime for which you have not been arrested? ☐ Yes ☐ No
   b. been arrested, cited, charged, indicted, fined, or imprisoned for breaking or violating any law or ordinance, excluding traffic violations? ☐ Yes ☐ No
   c. been the beneficiary of a pardon, amnesty, rehabilitation decree, other act of clemency or similar action? ☐ Yes ☐ No

2. Have you been convicted of any felony or 3 or more misdemeanors committed in the United States? ☐ Yes ☐ No

3. Have you ever exercised diplomatic immunity to avoid prosecution for a criminal offense in the U. S.? ☐ Yes ☐ No

4. Have you received public assistance from any source, including the U.S. government or any state, county, city, or municipality; or are you likely to request public assistance in the future? ☐ Yes ☐ No

5. Do you have, or have you ever had, a mental or physical disorder which does or may pose a threat to yourself or others? ☐ Yes ☐ No

6. Have you ever:
   a. practiced polygamy or plan to practice polygamy? ☐ Yes ☐ No
   b. within the past 10 years been a prostitute or procured anyone for prostitution, or intend to engage in such activities? ☐ Yes ☐ No
   c. engaged in any unlawful commercialized vice, including, but not limited to, gambling? ☐ Yes ☐ No
   d. knowingly encouraged, induced, assisted, abetted or aided, any alien to try to enter the U.S. illegally? ☐ Yes ☐ No
   e. illicitly trafficked in any controlled substance, or knowingly assisted, abetted or colluded in the illicit trafficking of any controlled substance? ☐ Yes ☐ No

7. Have you ever engaged in, conspired to engage in, or intend to engage in, or ever solicited membership or funds for, or through any means ever assisted or provided any type of material support to, any person or organization that has ever engaged or conspired to engage, in:
   a. sabotage, espionage, hijacking, or any other form of terrorist activity? ☐ Yes ☐ No
   b. any activity a purpose of which is opposition to, or the control of overthrow of, the Government of the United States, by force, violence or other unlawful means? ☐ Yes ☐ No
   c. any activity to violate or evade any law prohibiting the export from the United States of goods, technology or sensitive information? ☐ Yes ☐ No

8. Have you ever been, a member of, or in any way affiliated with, the Communist Party or any other totalitarian party? ☐ Yes ☐ No

9. Did you, during the period March 23, 1933 to May 8, 1945, in association with either the Nazi Government of Germany or any organization or government associated or allied with the Nazi Government of Germany, ever order, incite, assist or otherwise participate in the persecution of any person because of race, religion, national origin or political opinion? ☐ Yes ☐ No

10. Have you ever engaged in genocide, or otherwise ordered, incited, assisted or otherwise participated in the killing of any person because of race, religion, national origin or political opinion? ☐ Yes ☐ No

11. Have you ever been excluded from the U.S. within the past year, ever been deported from the U.S., or ever been removed from the U.S. at government expense, or are you now in exclusion or deportation proceedings? ☐ Yes ☐ No

12. Are you under a final order of civil penalty for violating section 274C of the Immigration Act for use of fraudulent documents, or have you, by fraud or willful misrepresentation of a material fact, ever sought to procure, or procured, a visa, other documentation, entry into the U.S., or any other immigration benefit? ☐ Yes ☐ No

13. Have you ever left the U.S. to avoid being drafted into the U.S. Armed Forces? ☐ Yes ☐ No

Form I-817 (Rev. 09-10-91)N   **Continued on back**

Figure 13: (cont.)

Part 4. Processing Information *(con't).*

14. Have you ever been a J nonimmigrant exchange visitor who was subject to the 2 year foreign residence requirement and not yet complied with that requirement? ☐ Yes ☐ No

15. Are you now withholding custody of a child outside the U.S. from a person granted custody of the child? ☐ Yes ☐ No

Part 5. Complete only if legalized alien is your spouse.

Section 1. *Additional Information about you, the applicant.*

Home Phone (   )   Work Phone   (   )

List all other names used (i.e. maiden name, aliases)

Sex: ☐ Male   ☐ Female   Number of Prior Marriages: _____

Section 2. *Additional Information about your legalized alien spouse.*

Home Phone of Legalized Alien   (   )   Work Phone of Legalized Alien   (   )

List all other names used (i.e. maiden name, aliases)

Sex: ☐ Male   ☐ Female   Number of Prior Marriages: _____

Section 3. *Information about your marriage.*

We were married on: *(date)*   /   /   We were married in *(City, U.S. State or Country)*

Type of Ceremony: ☐ Religious   ☐ Civil   ☐ None   We are: ☐ Now living together   ☐ Not living together

We are or intend to:*(Check one)*	**We have the following Joint Financial Assets or Contracts:** *(Check one)*
☐ Live together in a home or apartment	☐ Checking and/or Savings account
☐ Live together with my family	☐ Lease for apartment we occupy
☐ Live together with my spouse's family	☐ Mortgage for home we occupy
☐ Live together with non-relatives	☐ Credit cards
☐ Live separately from each other	☐ Consumer Loans

List three people (such as relatives, friends neighbors, co-workers, or employers) who know of your relationship:

	Name	Relationship	How long known
1.	Address		Phone number
2.	Name	Relationship	How long known
	Address		Phone number
3.	Name	Relationship	How long known
	Address		Phone number

Form I-817 (Rev. 09-10-91)N

Continued on back

Figure 13: (cont.)

52

Part 6. Complete only if you are the child of a legalized alien.

Sex: ☐ Male ☐ Female	Are you married? ☐ Yes ☐ No

My legalized alien parent is my: *(check one)*

☐ biological mother

☐ biological father who was married to my mother when I was born

☐ biological father who was not married to my mother when I was born

☐ adoptive parent:

    1. Did the adoption occur before your 16th birthday?   ☐ Yes ☐ No

    2. Did your parent have custody of you for at least 2-years after the adoption?   ☐ Yes ☐ No

    3. Did you live with your parent for at least 2 years after the adoption?   ☐ Yes ☐ No

☐ stepparent based on marriage to my parent which occurred before my 18th birthday.

☐ parent based on circumstances not described above *(explain in detail on separate paper).*

Part 7. Signature. *(Read the information on penalties in the instructions before completing this part. You must file this application while in the United States.)*

I certify under penalty of perjury under the laws of the United States of America that this application, and the evidence submitted with it, is all true and correct. I authorize the release of any information from my records which the Immigration and Naturalization Service needs to determine eligibility for the benefit I am seeking

Signature	*Print Your Name*	*Date*

Address

Part 8. Signature of person preparing form if other than above. *(Sign Below)*

I declare that I prepared this application at the request of the above person and it is based on all information of which I have knowledge.

Signature	Print Your Name	Date	Day time Phone Number

Firm Name
and Address

Form I-817 (Rev 09/10/91)N   For sale by the U.S. Government Printing Office
Superintendent of Documents, Mail Stop: SSOP, Washington, DC 20402-9328

Figure 13: (cont.)

Some Questions You May Have

How do I legalize my status?

If you have been living here for some time and feel you may not be eligible to become a citizen, do not give up hope. Under the Immigration Reform and Control Act of 1986, you may have already filed for temporary residence under the amnesty provisions. But even if you missed the date for filing, there are ways of adjusting, or legalizing, your status. In either case, if you are eligible to change from a temporary to a permanent resident, you may obtain Form I-485 or other appropriate forms by calling the Immigration and Naturalization Service at 1-800-870-3676 (free call). The fee for filing is $220. (See "Forms and Fees" section.)

What about my children?

Your natural children here with you may become citizens when you do if they are minors (under 18 years of age).

I am not sure that I have *continuous* residence because I went back and forth to Italy during my mother's illness. Do I qualify?

Try! But make sure you have filled in the form truthfully. Each case is judged on its merits.

Can I bring any of my family here?

When you become a permanent resident, you can petition for many family members. (See Form I-130 in "Forms and Fees" section.) When you become a citizen, you can do even more.

What is a Declaration of Intention?

Before 1952, people were required to file a Declaration of Intention to become a citizen of the United States. This paper used to be the "first paper." After filing the declaration, applicants had to wait at least two years before taking the next step—filing the Application for Naturalization. Now, filing the application is the first step in the naturalization process, which may be taken as soon as the alien has the required residence and the other qualifications for citizenship.

However, the law permits a Declaration of Intention to be filed if the applicant wishes to do so. This may be done any time after lawful admission to the United States. The form, N-300, may be obtained by calling the Immigration and Naturalization Service (INS) at 1-800-870-3676 and can be filed in the nearest court. The applicant must be 18 years or older. *There are no educational requirements* for obtaining this paper.

Why would I want to file a Declaration of Intention?

It might be needed in order to get a job or to obtain a license.

What is the difference between a Declaration of Intention and a Declaration of Intending Citizen?

The latter (Form I-772) applies to special groups of aliens, including refugees and those seeking asylum. Neither form is required for naturalization.

What can I do if I lose any of my naturalization papers or change my name?

A person whose Declaration of Intention or Certificate of Citizenship has been lost, mutilated, or destroyed or a naturalized person whose name has been changed by a court or by marriage *after* naturalization may apply for a new paper. The application form (N-565) is available from the INS Forms Line at 1-800-870-3676. It should be filled out, following the instructions on the form, and be taken or mailed to the local INS office, along with the required photographs and a check or money order for $135. Any documents that show the reason for the change of status should be submitted.

NOTE: If a person changes his or her name or marital status, there is no legal requirement to apply for a new certificate. This is the person's option.

If a person loses an Alien Registration Receipt Card (green card), he or she must file Form I-90. This form is also available from the INS Forms Line at 1-800-870-3676. Again it should be carefully filled out, following the instructions on the form, and submitted with a check or money order for $110 to that office.

Step 2— Filing Your Form

You have completed the sample forms. How do they look? Are they neat? If you needed to send them to the Immigration and Naturalization Service (INS), would you be proud to do so?

Have you received the forms that you need to fill in? If so, then you are ready to go on to the real thing!

How you fill out each form is very important. You want very much to become an American citizen; therefore, you must do your best in applying for citizenship.

All forms must be printed by hand or typewritten. Some forms have several copies and care must be taken that even the last copy can be read. All necessary documents should be included and they should be originals. If you want the original of any document back, have a copy made and submit it with the original. Then, when the immigration officer has checked it, the original will be returned to you and the copy kept with your application.

Form N-400: Now Fill Out the Real Thing

First, take out your Permanent Resident Card. Your name, exactly as it is on the card, must be printed in Part 1. Be careful as you fill in your alien registration number and your social security number. If you are using a *different name* now, of if you used any other name in the past, that goes in Part 3.

When you have completed your final form, you should mail it, with payment, to the appropriate regional office listed below. You may send it 3 months before you have the full residence time needed for your application. Include a check or money order for $250 made out to the Immigration and Naturalization Service. ($225 is the application fee, and $25 is the fingerprinting fee.) Also send in a copy of both sides of your Permanent Resident Card and two recent color photographs. Make copies of your N-400. Keep your copies in a safe place. Now mail "the real thing" and wait. You will hear from the INS telling you where and when to go to be fingerprinted.

Here is the list of regional offices:

If you live in Alabama, Arkansas, Florida, Georgia, Kentucky, Louisiana, Mississippi, New Mexico, North Carolina, Oklahoma, South Carolina, Tennessee, or Texas, send your application to:

> Texas Service Center
> P.O. Box 851204
> Mesquite, TX 75185-1204

If you live in Arizona, California, Hawaii, Nevada, Territory of Guam, or the Commonwealth of the Northern Mariana Islands, send your application to:

> California Service Center
> P.O. Box 10400
> Laguna Niguel, CA 92607-0400

If you live in Alaska, Colorado, Idaho, Illinois, Indiana, Iowa, Kansas, Michigan, Minnesota, Missouri, Montana, Nebraska, North Dakota, Ohio, Oregon, South Dakota, Utah, Washington, Wisconsin, or Wyoming, send your application to:

> Nebraska Service Center
> P.O. Box 87400
> Lincoln, NE 68501-7400

If you live in Connecticut, Delaware, Maine, Maryland, Massachusetts, New Hampshire, New Jersey, New York, Pennsylvania, Rhode Island, Vermont, Virginia, Washington D.C., West Virginia, Commonwealth of Puerto Rico, or the U.S. Virgin Islands, send your application to:

> Vermont Service Center
> 75 Lower Weldon Street
> St. Alban, VT 05479-0001

Note: If you are overseas and filing an N-400, you should send your application to the Service Center that serves the INS office where you want to be interviewed. For example, if you want to be interviewed in the Honolulu office, you should send your application to the California Service Center.

Important! Look for your state. Where will you mail your N-400?

Read this and answer: Where did Ann mail her form?

Let's see what one of my students did. She was very excited! Telling the class "It is time!" 3 months before she reached the 5 years residence required, Ann was ready to mail in her final form N-400. She made copies of it after she checked everything carefully, and she addressed it to the regional center that would take care of it. During the time that she had been a legal permanent resident of the United States, she had not moved from her home in Brooklyn, New York. Even though she plans to move after 3 months, she put her current address on the form she would mail. When she moves, she will have to notify INS. She will call the free number (1-800-870-3676) to request Form AR-11 (Alien's Change of Address Card) and mail it to the office where she sent her N-400. She knows it is very important to do that. If she does not do so, INS will not send her notification to the right address. For instance, she will not receive information on where to go to get fingerprinted, and she will not be aware of the date and place of her interview.

START HERE - Please Type or Print

Part 1. Information about you.

Family Name	Given Name	Middle Initial

U.S. Mailing Address - Care of

Street Number and Name		Apt. #

City	County

State	ZIP Code

Date of Birth (month/day/year)	Country of Birth

Social Security #	A #

Part 2. Basis for Eligibility (check one).

a. ☐ I have been a permanent resident for at least five (5) years

b. ☐ I have been a permanent resident for at least three (3) years and have been married to a United States Citizen for those three years.

c. ☐ I am a permanent resident child of United States citizen parent(s)

d. ☐ I am applying on the basis of qualifying military service in the Armed Forces of the U.S. and have attached completed Forms N-426 and G-325B

e. ☐ Other. (Please specify section of law) _____

Part 3. Additional information about you.

Date you became a permanent resident (month/day/year)	Port admitted with an immmigrant visa or INS Office where granted adjustment of status.

Citizenship

Name on alien registration card (if different than in Part 1)

Other names used since you became a permanent resident (including maiden name)

Sex	☐ Male ☐ Female	Height	Marital Status:	☐ Single ☐ Married	☐ Divorced ☐ Widowed

Can you speak, read and write English ? ☐No ☐Yes.

Absences from the U.S.:

Have you been absent from the U.S. since becoming a permanent resident? ☐ No ☐Yes.

If you answered **"Yes"** , complete the following. Begin with your most recent absence. If you need more room to explain the reason for an absence or to list more trips, continue on separate paper.

Date left U.S.	Date returned	Did absence last 6 months or more?	Destination	Reason for trip
		☐ Yes ☐ No		
		☐ Yes ☐ No		
		☐ Yes ☐ No		
		☐ Yes ☐ No		
		☐ Yes ☐ No		
		☐ Yes ☐ No		

Form N-400 (Rev. 07/17/91)N   *Continued on back.*

FOR INS USE ONLY

Returned	Receipt

Resubmitted

Reloc Sent

Reloc Rec'd

☐ Applicant Interviewed

At interview

☐ request naturalization ceremony at court

Remarks

Action

To Be Completed by *Attorney or Representative*, if any
☐ Fill in box if G-28 is attached to represent the applicant

VOLAG#

ATTY State License #

Part 4. Information about your residences and employment.

A. List your addresses during the last five (5) years or since you became a permanent resident, whichever is less. Begin with your current address. If you need more space, continue on separate paper:

Street Number and Name, City, State, Country, and Zip Code	Dates (month/day/year)	
	From	To

B. List your employers during the last five (5) years. List your present or most recent employer first. If none, write "None". If you need more space, continue on separate paper.

Employer's Name	Employer's Address	Dates Employed (month/day/year)		Occupation/position
	Street Name and Number - City, State and ZIP Code	From	To	

Part 5. Information about your marital history.

A. Total number of times you have been married _____ If you are now married, complete the following regarding your husband or wife.

Family name	Given name	Middle initial

Address

Date of birth (month/day/year)	Country of birth	Citizenship
Social Security#	A# (if applicable)	Immigration status (If not a U.S. citizen)

Naturalization (If applicable)
(month/day/year)   Place   (City, State)

If you have ever previously been married or if your current spouse has been previously married, please provide the following on separate paper: Name of prior spouse, date of marriage, date marriage ended, how marriage ended and immigration status of prior spouse.

Part 6. Information about your children.

B. Total Number of Children _____ Complete the following information for each of your children. If the child lives with you, state "with me" in the address column; otherwise give city/state/country of child's current residence. If deceased, write "deceased" in the address column. If you need more space, continue on separate paper.

Full name of child	Date of birth	Country of birth	Citizenship	A - Number	Address

Form N-400 (Rev 07/17/91)N

Continued on next page

Part 7. Additional eligibility factors.

Please answer each of the following questions. If your answer is **"Yes"**, explain on a separate paper.

1. Are you now, or have you ever been a member of, or in any way connected or associated with the Communist Party, or ever knowingly aided or supported the Communist Party directly, or indirectly through another organization, group or person, or ever advocated, taught, believed in, or knowingly supported or furthered the interests of communism? ☐ Yes ☐ No

2. During the period March 23, 1933 to May 8, 1945, did you serve in, or were you in any way affiliated with, either directly or indirectly, any military unit, paramilitary unit, police unit, self-defense unit, vigilante unit, citizen unit of the Nazi party or SS, government agency or office, extermination camp, concentration camp, prisoner of war camp, prison, labor camp, detention camp or transit camp, under the control or affiliated with:
   a. The Nazi Government of Germany? ☐ Yes ☐ No
   b. Any government in any area occupied by, allied with, or established with the assistance or cooperation of, the Nazi Government of Germany? ☐ Yes ☐ No

3. Have you at any time, anywhere, ever ordered, incited, assisted, or otherwise participated in the persecution of any person because of race, religion, national origin, or political opinion? ☐ Yes ☐ No

4. Have you ever left the United States to avoid being drafted into the U.S. Armed Forces? ☐ Yes ☐ No

5. Have you ever failed to comply with Selective Service laws? ☐ Yes ☐ No
   If you have registered under the Selective Service laws, complete the following information:
   Selective Service Number: _____ Date Registered: _____
   If you registered before 1978, also provide the following:
   Local Board Number: _____ Classification: _____

6. Did you ever apply for exemption from military service because of alienage, conscientious objections or other reasons? ☐ Yes ☐ No

7. Have you ever deserted from the military, air or naval forces of the United States? ☐ Yes ☐ No

8. Since becoming a permanent resident, have you ever failed to file a federal income tax return? ☐ Yes ☐ No

9. Since becoming a permanent resident, have you filed a federal income tax return as a nonresident or failed to file a federal return because you considered yourself to be a nonresident? ☐ Yes ☐ No

10. Are deportation proceedings pending against you, or have you ever been deported, or ordered deported, or have you ever applied for suspension of deportation? ☐ Yes ☐ No

11. Have you ever claimed in writing, or in any way, to be a United States citizen? ☐ Yes ☐ No

12. Have you ever:
   a. been a habitual drunkard? ☐ Yes ☐ No
   b. advocated or practiced polygamy? ☐ Yes ☐ No
   c. been a prostitute or procured anyone for prostitution? ☐ Yes ☐ No
   d. knowingly and for gain helped any alien to enter the U.S. illegally? ☐ Yes ☐ No
   e. been an illicit trafficker in narcotic drugs or marijuana? ☐ Yes ☐ No
   f. received income from illegal gambling? ☐ Yes ☐ No
   g. given false testimony for the purpose of obtaining any immigration benefit? ☐ Yes ☐ No

13. Have you ever been declared legally incompetent or have you ever been confined as a patient in a mental institution? ☐ Yes ☐ No

14. Were you born with, or have you acquired in same way, any title or order of nobility in any foreign State? ☐ Yes ☐ No

15. Have you ever:
   a. knowingly committed any crime for which you have not been arrested? ☐ Yes ☐ No
   b. been arrested, cited, charged, indicted, convicted, fined or imprisoned for breaking or violating any law or ordinance excluding traffic regulations? ☐ Yes ☐ No

(If you answer yes to 15, in your explanation give the following information for each incident or occurrence the **city**, **state**, and **country**, where the offense took place, the **date** and **nature** of the offense, and the **outcome** or **disposition** of the case).

Part 8. Allegiance to the U.S.

If your answer to any of the following questions is **"NO"**, attach a full explanation:

1. Do you believe in the Constitution and form of government of the U.S.? ☐ Yes ☐ No
2. Are you willing to take the full Oath of Allegiance to the U.S.? (see instructions) ☐ Yes ☐ No
3. If the law requires it, are you willing to bear arms on behalf of the U.S.? ☐ Yes ☐ No
4. If the law requires it, are you willing to perform noncombatant services in the Armed Forces of the U.S.? ☐ Yes ☐ No
5. If the law requires it, are you willing to perform work of national importance under civilian direction? ☐ Yes ☐ No

Form N-400 (Rev 07/17/91)N

Continued on back

Part 9. Memberships and organizations.

A. List your present and past membership in or affiliation with every organization, association, fund, foundation, party, club, society, or similar group in the United States or in any other place. Include any military service in this part. If none, write "none". Include the name of organization, location, dates of membership and the nature of the organization. If additional space is needed, use separate paper.

_____

_____

_____

_____

Part 10. Complete only if you checked block " C " in Part 2.

How many of your parents are U.S. citizens?   ☐ One   ☐ Both   (Give the following about one U.S. citizen parent:)

Family Name	Given Name	Middle Name

Address _____

Basis for citizenship:	Relationship to you (check one):	☐ natural parent	☐ adoptive parent
☐ Birth			
☐ Naturalization Cert. No.		☐ parent of child legitimated after birth	

If adopted or legitimated after birth, give date of adoption or, legitimation: _(month/day/year)_ _____

Does this parent have legal custody of you?   ☐ Yes   ☐ No

(Attach a copy of relating evidence to establish that you are the child of this U.S. citizen and evidence of this parent's citizenship.)

Part 11. Signature.   _(Read the information on penalties in the instructions before completing this section)._

I certify or, if outside the United States, I swear or affirm, under penalty of perjury under the laws of the United States of America that this application, and the evidence submitted with it, is all true and correct. I authorize the release of any information from my records which the Immigration and Naturalization Service needs to determine eligibility for the benefit I am seeking.

Signature _____   Date _____

Please Note: If you do not completely fill out this form, or fail to submit required documents listed in the instructions, you may not be found eligible for naturalization and this application may be denied.

Part 12. Signature of person preparing form if other than above. _(Sign below)_

I declare that I prepared this application at the request of the above person and it is based on all information of which I have knowledge.

Signature _____   Print Your Name _____   Date _____

Firm Name
and Address _____

DO NOT COMPLETE THE FOLLOWING UNTIL INSTRUCTED TO DO SO AT THE INTERVIEW

I swear that I know the contents of this application, and supplemental pages 1 through_____, that the corrections , numbered 1 through_____, were made at my request, and that this amended application, is true to the best of my knowledge and belief.

_____
(Complete and true signature of applicant)

Subscribed and sworn to before me by the applicant.

_____
(Examiner's Signature)   Date

Form N-400 (Rev 07/17/91)N

FPI-LOM

63

Probability Questions

Now that you have started the process, let's see where you are, as far as knowledge of your new country, its history, and the foundation of government here. Before you go on to the next step, read over the 25 questions and answers that follow. See how many are easy for you! I call them *probability questions* because it is probable that you will be asked some of them at your naturalization interview. While that may be a long way off, it is best to have some idea and some practice in using the words of the naturalization examiner. *Do not try to memorize them!* These are typical questions asked by the naturalization examiner and sample answers that are acceptable.

1. What is the form of government of the United States of America?

    It is a democracy and a republic, which means that it is a government of the people, by the people, and for the people.

2. How many states are there in the United States of America?
    Fifty.

3. What is the highest law of the United States of America?
    The Constitution.

4. What is the highest court of the United States of America?
    The Supreme Court.

5. Who is the president of the United States of America?
    Bill Clinton (as of January 2000).

6. Who was the first president of the United States of America?
    George Washington.

7. Who was the president who freed the slaves?
    Abraham Lincoln issued the Emancipation Proclamation.

8. Why do we celebrate the Fourth of July?
    The Fourth of July is Independence Day, the day the colonies declared their independence from England in 1776.

9. What are the colors of the American flag?
    Red, white, and blue.

10. Describe the flag.
    It has 13 stripes, one for each of the 13 original colonies; and it has 50 stars, one for each of the current states. The stars are white on a blue background.

11. Who makes the laws for the United States?
    Congress, made up of the Senate and the House of Representatives. The Senate has 100 members; the House of Representatives has 435.

12. What is the Supreme Court?

It is the highest court of the country. It interprets laws and declares unconstitutional any laws that are not in accordance with the Constitution. Such laws cannot remain in effect.

13. Can the Constitution be changed?

Yes, it can be changed by amendment.

14. What is the Bill of Rights?

The first 10 amendments to the Constitution that protect the rights of all Americans.

15. What is the Fourteenth Amendment?

This amendment, which took effect in 1868, provides important protection to all citizens. The first part of this amendment says: "All persons born or naturalized in the United States, and subject to the jurisdiction thereof, are citizens of the United States, and of the state wherein they reside. No State shall make or enforce any law which shall abridge the privileges or immunities of citizens of the United States; nor shall any State deprive any person of life, liberty, or property, without due process of law."

16. What is the difference between the Bill of Rights and the Fourteenth Amendment?

The Bill of Rights protects us from actions of the federal government, and the Fourteenth Amendment protects us from actions of the state as well.

17. Who is the chief executive of the United States?

The president.

18. Who is the chief executive of the state?

The governor.

19. Are there governments other than the federal government?

Yes. There are state and local governments.

20. What is meant by "checks and balances" in the government of the United States?

Each of the three departments of government has power to veto (or declare unconstitutional) the action of another. The Senate must approve some appointments made by the president. That is just one example.

21. How is the president elected?

By the people through the Electoral College, made up of representatives from each state. The candidate must receive a majority of votes in order to be elected.

22. What is the term of office of a president?

Four years.

23. What is the term of office of a senator? A congressman or -woman?

Six years for a senator. Two years for a congressman or -woman.

24. What is the cabinet?

The heads of the executive departments appointed by the president to advise him.

25. How many cabinet members are there, and what do they do?

There are 14, and they advise the president on special matters.

Step 3—Serious Study

Some time may pass between when you request the forms and when you file them. Use this time to become more familiar with the language of citizenship and naturalization.

Read the passages that follow until you feel you understand enough to answer the questions that appear in this section. It is best if you read this *aloud* and underline those words that you are unfamiliar with. Look them up either in the Word List at the back of this book or in a dictionary that gives pronunciation. Then work on the practice exercises.

As you read, speak slowly and carefully. It has been my experience that more people fail the naturalization examination because the examiner does not understand the applicant than because the applicant does not know the answer. If you are having difficulties pronouncing certain words, review the section on Pronunciation Practice in the Appendix. Practice makes perfect! You know you are working to get something that is important to you and your family, so do your best on the next section of this book.

Like the Pretest, this section will show you what you need to practice. Do the short exercise below for writing practice.

Print your full name here _____

Your address _____
          House number first   Zip Code

The date here _____

Your Permanent Resident Card number here _____

In your own words, write the answer to the question: How can I go from alien to citizen?

_____

_____

_____

_____

_____

_____

Check your answer with the information on page 22.

Practice Test of Written English

Test yourself on the requirements for naturalization by answering the questions in the spaces provided. This test will help you measure your progress. If you do well, continue to the next practice test. If you get several items wrong, review Part One.

To become a naturalized citizen of the United States:

1. How old must you be? _____

   _____

2. Do you have to be lawfully admitted to the United States? _____

   _____

3. Is there any residence requirement for naturalization? _____

   _____

4. Do you have to be able to speak English? _____

   _____

5. Do you have to be able to read and write English?_____

   _____

6. Do you have to be of good moral character? _____

   _____

7. Do you need to know some American history? _____

_____

8. Do you need to know what the Constitution is and how it protects you? _____

_____

9. Do you need to know how the government of the United States functions? _____

_____

10. Is there any exception to the requirement that you know the fundamentals of American history and government? _____

_____

Check your answers to these questions with the answer key on pags 210–211. If you have answered all of the preceding questions correctly, answer the next set of questions in the spaces provided. Otherwise, go back and review the sections of the book that pertain to the questions you did not know.

11. What is the first step in becoming a citizen of the United States? _

_____

12. What is meant by being lawfully admitted to this country? _____

_____

13. Why must you be very careful in filling out Form N-400? _____

_____

14. If you wish to change your name, may you do so? _____

_____

15. Why would anyone file a Declaration of Intention? _____

_____

If your answers agree with the answer key on page 211, continue on to the next questions. If not, go back and review the sections of the book that pertain to the questions you did not know.

16. What rights do citizens have that immigrants do not have? _____

_____

17. What is another name for an immigrant? _____

_____

18. Do immigrants live under the laws and Constitution of the United States?_____

_____

19. Can every person who enters the United States become a citizen? Explain._____

_____

20. Is every citizen a voter? Explain._____

_____

If your answers are correct (see the answer key on page 211), continue on to the next questions. If not, go back and review the sections of the book that pertain to the questions you did not know.

21. When can an immigrant file a petition for naturalization?_____

_____

22. Is any investigation of the applicant made before he or she becomes a citizen?_____

_____

23. Does the applicant have to take any test?_____

_____

24. Will this be difficult or easy? Explain._____

_____

25. Is there anything special to be done at the preliminary hearing?__

_____

If your answers are correct (see the answer key on page 211), fill in the blanks next to the questions. If not, go back and review the sections of the book that pertain to the questions you did not know.

26. The name of the governor of the state where I live is _____

_____

27. The two senators from this state are _____

and_____.

28. I live in the_____Congressional District.

29. The name of my representative is _____.

You Are Ready!

30. I want to become a citizen of the United States because_____

_____

31. I think it is important for a citizen to vote because _____

_____

Now, write the answer to this question in the space provided. Try to include at least three reasons. Be as specific as you can.

32. What is meant by good moral character? _____

_____

_____

_____

_____

_____

_____

_____

_____

_____

_____

Note that you must locate the answers to questions 26–31 yourself. The answer to question 32 may be found in Reading Practice I.

How many answers did you have correct in this Practice Test? Put the number here:_____

Reading Practice I

Now practice your oral English by reading this passage aloud.

Good Moral Character

In general, good moral character means that you act in accordance with society's principles of right or good conduct and that you are honest and ethical. The Immigration and Naturalization Service has given the following reasons for denial of citizenship:

- Illegal gambling
- Terrorist acts
- Drug or alcohol addiction
- Prostitution
- Criminal record during period of residence here or conviction for murder at any time
- Lying under oath in order to gain citizenship
- Polygamy (having more than one spouse at the same time)
- Failing to pay court-ordered child support or alimony payments

It is important to answer all questions relating to this subject truthfully!

Except for the crime of murder, the requirement of good moral character refers to the immigrant's behavior during his or her period of residence here. If your answer was similar to the following, it indicates that you understand what is acceptable behavior (action) and what is not acceptable.

Good moral character means that you know the difference between right and wrong, that you choose to obey the laws of the United States and to observe the standards of your new country.

HOW ARE YOU DOING?

Read each question aloud. Answer by writing "yes" or "no" on the line next to the question.

1. Have you at any time, anywhere, ever ordered, incited, assisted, or otherwise participated in the persecution of any person because of race, religion, national origin, or political opinion? _____

_____

2. Have you ever failed to comply with the Selective Service laws? __

_____

3. Since becoming a permanent resident, have you ever failed to file a Federal income tax return? _____

_____

4. Do you believe in the Constitution and form of government of the United States? _____

_____

5. Have you ever given false testimony for the purpose of obtaining any immigration benefit? _____

_____

Did you understand the questions?

Did you answer "no" to questions 1, 2, 3, and 5?

Did you answer "yes" to question 4?

You passed the test.

Practice saying these words:

assist	**service**	**participate**
persecute	**allegiance**	

Look them up in the Word List.

Reading Practice II

Now test your progress in oral English by reading and answering the questions following the reading passages. Read aloud in front of a mirror or have someone listen to your pronunciation.

Who Can Be Naturalized?

Men and women who have entered the United States for permanent residence, or who have qualified for amnesty under the terms of the 1986 Immigration Reform and Control Act, and who want to be citizens may apply for naturalization. Others have done it, and you can do it, too!

When we move from alien to citizen, we become equal to people who were born here or who were naturalized before us. No one asks how or when! We can start the process if we are 18 years or older, were legally accepted for permanent residence, and have lived here for five or more years. There are some exceptions to the residence requirement; and I know they are based on the immigration laws.

The first step to naturalization is to obtain and fill out an Application for Naturalization (Form N-400) and then mail it with a check or money order for $250 (which includes the fingerprinting fee) to the appropriate regional office of the Immigration and Naturalization Service. And then wait!

REVIEW

1. What do the following words mean?

amnesty	eligible	naturalization
application	exception	newcomer
apply	ineligible	requirement
basis	lawfully	residence
eligibility	legally	resident

How did you do?
Check your answers with the Word List at the back of this book.

2. Use each of the above words in a sentence.

For example: The *basis* for my *eligibility* is five years as a permanent *resident* of the United States.

Here, three words were used in the same sentence. Can you do the same? If you have difficulty, go back to Part One to find how the words were used there.

_____

_____

_____

_____

_____

_____

_____

_____

_____

_____

_____

_____

Reading Practice III

Read the passages out loud.

The Immigration Reform and Control Act (IRCA)

The Immigration Reform and Control Act (IRCA) took effect in November 1986 and it provided a new way to become naturalized. The act included legalization of some undocumented (without papers) aliens who entered this country before 1982 and applied for amnesty between May 5, 1987 and May 4, 1988. The word *amnesty* means a general pardon. In this case, people asked to be pardoned for entering, or remaining in the United States of America illegally, before January 1, 1982.

IRCA made it illegal for employers to hire illegal aliens. Employers who violate (break) the law may have to pay a very high fine (penalty). When considering whether to hire a worker, employers must ask for proof that the worker is "legal." If employers do not do so, they may have to pay a fine (penalty).

The Immigration Act of 1990

The current naturalization requirements are in accordance with the provisions of Public Law 101-649 (November 29, 1990) and the regulations adopted up to May 1999. Title IV of this law covers naturalization as the sole authority of the Attorney General of the United States. The only provision affecting persons filing form N-400 is that the law substitutes 3 months residence in the INS district for 6 months residence in a state, which was previously required. Everything in this book is in accordance with the present law.

There have been important changes in the law itself and in the rules and regulations set up by Congress since P.L. 101-649 was passed and signed into law by President Bush in 1990.

Some of the changes are increased fees for various forms included in the first section in this book. Other changes relate to the "green card lottery," to the adjustment of status regulation that has now ended, and to the barring of readmission for persons on unauthorized status for more than 6 months. If you have any questions other than how much the forms will cost, it is recommended that you check with one of the immigration service agencies or consult an attorney specializing in immigration law.

At this writing, other changes in the law are being contemplated. One change would reduce legal immigration by as much as 30%; another would limit the admission of adult children of legal immigrants. In an effort to stop illegal immigration, border patrols have already been increased.

Watch for these changes even though they will not affect you who have applied because these changes may limit your ability to bring in relatives!

Review: More Writing Practice

Read each question carefully. Then write your answers in the spaces provided. Read your answer out loud to see if it makes sense. You can check what you wrote with the answers on the next page.

1. In your own words, write the answer to the question "What is naturalization?" _____

   _____

   _____

   _____

2. In your own words, write the answer to the question "Why is it important for me to go through the naturalization process?" _____

   _____

   _____

   _____

   _____

   _____

   _____

Now turn the book upside down and compare your answers with the answers given below. If you left something out, write the answer again, either below this sentence, or on another sheet of paper. If you wrote the answer using different words, you may still be correct. However, the main meaning of these answers must be the same. If not, write both question and correct answer on a separate sheet of paper.

Acceptable Answers

1. Naturalization is the process of becoming a citizen, or the act of going from *alien* to *citizen.*

2. I want to be able to *vote.* I also think it is important to get an American *passport,* and to help some of my relatives come into the United States of America so our family is not separated. It may also enable me to apply for a government job or to be *elected* to public office. And it will not be necessary for me to show a *card* to prove that I belong here!

Step 4—Serious Study—History and Civics

Part One included the *main requirements* for naturalization. There are also two *educational requirements* for naturalization.

The *first educational requirement* is that you understand English and be able to read, write, and speak words in ordinary use. Remember: Only those persons who are physically unable to do this, or persons over 50 years old who have lived in the United States as permanent residents for over 20 years, or who are over 55 with more than 15 years of residence, are excused from this requirement. Step 3 gave you practice in reading and writing words needed to meet this educational requirement.

In Step 4, you will also learn the facts that you need in order to meet the *second educational requirement* for naturalization: to demonstrate a knowledge and understanding of the history, principles, and form of government of the United States (civics). An applicant who has a physical or developmental disability or a mental impairment may be exempt from this requirement.

Note: This is a self-help book. While you are learning important facts, each unit aims to help you improve your English. Pay attention to words and their meaning while you read and learn the content in Step 4. You will learn all you need to know—and much more!

Our Government

Our government is a **democracy.** That means it is a government of the people, by the people, and for the people. It is a government by the elected representatives of all the voters. It is a *tripartite* government, which means it has three parts, or branches.

Our government is also a **republic.** This means that the supreme power is given to representatives elected by popular vote of all citizens.

You see that democracy and republic mean almost the same thing. Long ago, in small units of government, citizens got together and made the laws for their communities. That is the real meaning of democracy. Today that kind of democracy exists only in a few small towns in the northeastern part of our country. Through town meetings, all of the voters decide on what is to be done in their town.

Of course, this is not possible where a great many people live. Today, we make our voices heard by voting for people to represent us. The two largest political parties in the United States, the Democratic and the Republican parties, derive their names from *democracy* and *republic;* so it should not be difficult to remember these words.

Our country is a **federation,** or association, of states. The government for the whole country is, therefore, called the *federal government*. The plan for this government is set by the Constitution, the supreme law of our land.

Remember: The government is divided into three branches—the legislative, the executive, and the judicial. That is why it is called a *tripartite* government.

You Are Ready!

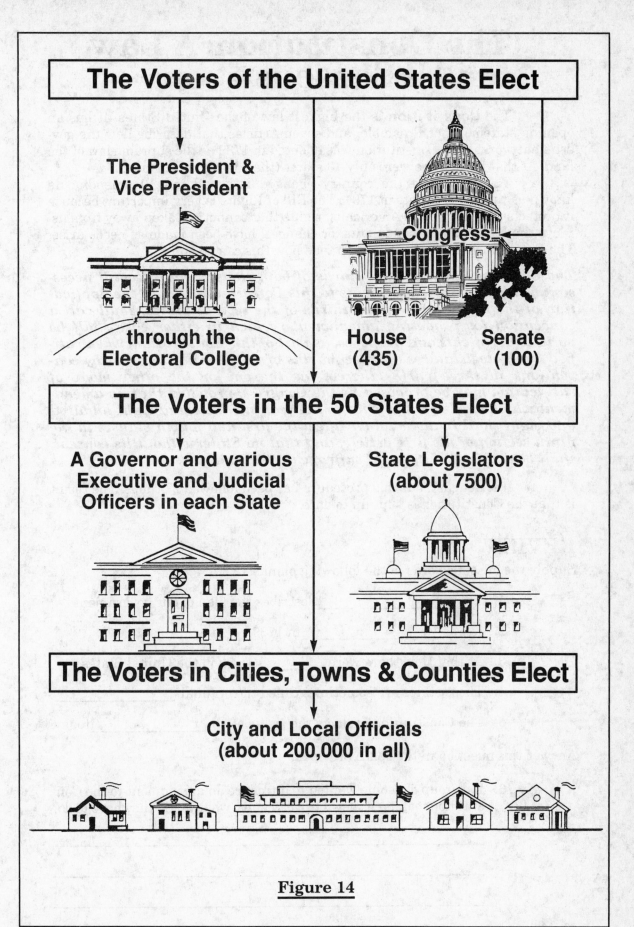

The Voters of the United States Elect

The President & Vice President

Congress

through the Electoral College

House (435)   **Senate (100)**

The Voters in the 50 States Elect

A Governor and various Executive and Judicial Officers in each State

State Legislators (about 7500)

The Voters in Cities, Towns & Counties Elect

City and Local Officials (about 200,000 in all)

<u>Figure 14</u>

Source: U.S. Department of Justice, Immigration and Naturalization Service

The Constitution: A Law for All Seasons

The **Constitution** is the highest law of the United States. It has an opening statement, or Preamble, and seven Articles that describe how the government works. The Constitution was adopted in 1789 as the supreme law of the land. At that time, there were only 13 states (the 13 original colonies).

The leaders of the country changed it by adding 10 amendments known as the Bill of Rights in 1791. The Bill of Rights is very important because it protects the rights of all Americans, rights that cannot be taken away from us. Since that time other amendments, or changes, have been made as needs arise. The Fifth Article of the Constitution tells how this can be done:

The Congress, whenever two-thirds of both Houses shall deem it necessary, shall propose amendments to this Constitution, or, on the application of the legislatures of two-thirds of the several States, shall call a convention for proposing amendments, which in either case shall be valid to all intents and purposes, as part of this Constitution, when ratified by the legislatures of three-fourths of the several States, or by conventions in three-fourths thereof, as the one or the other mode of ratification may be proposed by the Congress; provided that no amendment which may be made prior to the year one thousand eight hundred and eight shall in any manner affect the first and fourth clauses in the ninth section of the first article; and that no State, without its consent, shall be deprived of its equal suffrage in the Senate.

It is not easy, but this procedure has been followed 27 times. The result is that the Constitution is kept up to date.

REVIEW

Supply the missing words in the following blanks.

1. The_____describes the plan of our government.

2. It was_____in 1789.

3. At that time there were_____states in the United States.

4. These states are sometimes called the original _____

5. The Constitution protects the rights of all_____today.

Answer this question in the space provided.

6. If a group of people wanted to introduce an amendment to the Constitution making it illegal to carry guns, what would they have to do?

_____

_____

_____

See the answer key on page 212.

THE CONSTITUTION AS IT WAS ADOPTED

Preamble (Introduction)

Explains the purposes of the people in adopting the Constitution.

First Article

Provides for a Congress and defines its power to make laws.

Second Article

Provides for the election of a President and Vice President, with defined powers, and for the *appointment* of other officials.

Third Article

Sets up a Supreme Court, authorizes the Congress to set up other courts, and defines their powers.

Fourth Article

Defines relationships between the Federal Government and the States, and between the States themselves.

Fifth Article

Tells how the Constitution may be amended.

Sixth Article

Accepts responsibility for all debts that the Nation owed before the adoption of the Constitution; declares that the Constitution, constitutional laws, and treaties are the supreme law of the land; and provides that all public officers must take an oath to support the Constitution.

Seventh Article

Declares that ratification (approval) by nine States will put the Constitution into effect.

Figure 15

Source: U.S. Department of Justice, Immigration and Naturalization Service

THE BILL OF RIGHTS—1791

First Amendment

Forbids the Congress to interfere with religion, free speech, a free press,
or with the right to *assemble* peaceably, or to petition the Government.

Second Amendment

Guarantees to the people the right to have weapons.

Third Amendment

Guarantees against lodging soldiers in private houses without the
consent of the owners.

Fourth Amendment

Provides that there shall be no search or *seizure* of persons,
houses, goods, or papers, without a *warrant*.

Fifth Amendment

Declares that there shall be no *trial* for serious offenses without a *grand
jury indictment*, no repeated trials for the same offense, no *condemnation*
without trial, no compulsion to be a *witness* against oneself, and no
property taken for public use except at a fair price.

Sixth Amendment

Requires a speedy and public trial for criminal offenses in the district where the
crime was committed, a fair jury, a plain statement of the *accusation*, gives the
accused the right to be represented by a lawyer and to *compel* the attendance of
his witnesses, and requires all witnesses to *testify* in the presence of the accused.

Seventh Amendment

Provides that in *lawsuits* about anything valued at more than $20,
a trial by jury shall be allowed.

Eighth Amendment

Prohibits too large *bail* or *fines*, and cruel or unusual *punishments*.

Ninth Amendment

Declares that rights not stated in the Constitution are not
therefore taken away from the people.

Tenth Amendment

States that powers not delegated to the United States nor prohibited by the
Constitution to the States are reserved to the States or to the people.

<u>Figure 16</u>

Source: U.S. Department of Justice, Immigration and Naturalization Service

AMENDMENTS PASSED AFTER THE BILL OF RIGHTS

Eleventh Amendment (1795)
A citizen of one state, or an alien, cannot sue another state in a Federal court.

Twelfth Amendment (1804)
Electors must vote for President and Vice President separately.

Thirteenth Amendment (1865)
Ended slavery.

Fourteenth Amendment (1868)
All persons born or naturalized in the United States are citizens.

Fifteenth Amendment (1870)
No person can be kept from voting because of race or color.

Sixteenth Amendment (1913)
Congress has the power to put a tax on money earned by the people.

Seventeenth Amendment (1913)
Senators are to be elected by the people.

Eighteenth Amendment (1919)
Prohibited the making, selling or transportation of intoxicating liquor.

Nineteenth Amendment (1920)
No person can be kept from voting because of being a woman.

Twentieth Amendment (1933)
The President, the Vice President, and the Congress shall take office in January.

Twenty-first Amendment (1933)
Did away with the Eighteenth Amendment.

Twenty-second Amendment (1951)
The same person cannot be elected President more than twice.

Twenty-third Amendment (1961)
Citizens living in the District of Columbia can vote for
President and Vice President.

Twenty-fourth Amendment (1964)
Citizens cannot be made to pay a tax to vote for the President,
the Vice President or members of the Congress.

Twenty-fifth Amendment (1967)
The Vice President becomes Acting President when the President is disabled.

Twenty-sixth Amendment (1971)
A citizen shall not be denied the right to vote because of age
if he is eighteen years of age or older.

Twenty-seventh Amendment (1992)
Compensation for the services of Senators and Representatives
shall not be changed until an election is held.

Figure 17

Source: U.S. Department of Justice, Immigration and Naturalization Service

FOUR WAYS OF AMENDING OUR
FEDERAL CONSTITUTION

**AMENDMENTS MAY BE
PROPOSED BY—**

**AND *TAKE EFFECT* WHEN
RATIFIED BY—**

THE CONGRESS
(By favorable vote of
two-thirds of those vot-
ing in both houses.)

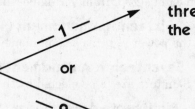

— 1 —

or

— 2 —

The *legislatures* of
three-fourths of all
the States.

Special State conven-
tions in three-fourths
of all the States.

**A NATIONAL
CONVENTION**
(Called by Congress
when requested by
two-thirds of the State
legislatures.)

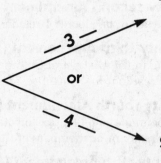

— 3 —

or

— 4 —

The legislatures of
three-fourths of all
the States.

Special State conven-
tions in three-fourths
of all the States.

<u>Figure 18</u>

Source: U.S. Department of Justice, Immigration and Naturalization Service

Reading Practice

Practice your oral English by reading the passage below. Then check your understanding by writing about what you have read in the spaces provided.

The Government of the United States

The government of the United States of America is a democracy, a government of the people, by the people, and for the people. It is a tripartite government because it has three parts, or branches. (*Tri* means three.) You know that a triangle has three sides. In the same way, our government has three branches.

These branches are the legislative, or law-making, the executive, and the judicial. The executive branch carries out the laws. The judicial branch judges laws.

The plan of our government is in the Constitution, the highest law of the land. When the Constitution was first written, the leaders of the new country left out the rights of the people. This was an oversight for the citizens wanting a guarantee that their rights would be protected. And so, the first 10 amendments to the Constitution were adopted to do just that. They are called the Bill of Rights.

These rights are listed on page 82. Read them again! Then write a summary of them in your own words on the lines below. Check to see how your summary agrees with paragraph number three on page 86.

_____

_____

_____

_____

_____

_____

_____

_____

_____

Summary: How the Bill of Rights Protects Americans

1. The first 10 amendments to the Constitution are called the Bill of Rights.

2. These rights are guaranteed by the Constitution, the highest law of our land, and are protected by the Supreme Court, the highest court of our land. The amendments were adopted in 1791 and now are over 200 years old. They are still used to protect us.

3. These amendments include: freedom of religion, of speech, and of the press; the right to assemble peacefully and to petition (ask) the government to set right or cancel a law that denies them their rights. The Bill of Rights also guarantees that no one will come into your house to search it without a warrant. And we have the right to bear arms (carry guns) to protect ourselves, as well as the right to a fair trial if we are accused of a crime. The last amendment, the 10th, states that any power not given to the federal government is a power of the state or the people. (We will read more about this in the section on state and local governments.)

4. Sometimes, we hear of a witness in a court trial, "taking the Fifth." This refers to the Fifth Amendment, "no person shall be compelled to be a witness against himself, nor be deprived of life, liberty or property without due process of law."

5. Another important guarantee of "due process" is in the Fourteenth Amendment, which was adopted in 1868 after the Civil War. The Fourteenth Amendment also tells us the meaning of the word citizen:

"All persons born or naturalized in the United States, and subject to its jurisdiction [authority] are citizens of the United States, and of the state where they reside. . ."

PRACTICE
Answer these questions in your own words.

1. Why is it important that the rights of all the people are protected?

_____

_____

Check your answer with the summary above.

2. What is meant by due process of law? _____

_____

_____

Check your answer with the Word List at the back of this book.

The Federal Government: Form and Structure

The Constitution broadly outlines the form and structure of the federal government. Details of operation and management have been worked out over the years since 1789, so that what we have today is a workable system of government for 50 states.

The writers of the Constitution set up the government in such a way that no person, or group of persons, would have too much power. Our system of government is based on two principles: the *separation of powers* and a system of *checks and balances*. Let us see what these principles mean.

The government is divided into three branches—the legislative, the executive, and the judicial—each with separate functions.

The **legislative branch,** or **Congress,** makes the laws. It is composed of a Senate and a House of Representatives. Two senators are elected from each state, each for a six-year term; representatives are elected for terms of two years. The number of representatives each state has is determined by the size of its population.

The **executive branch** is headed by the president, who is elected for a term of four years. A vice president is elected at the same time and from the same political party. The Constitution tells how a president may be removed from office. It provides that upon such removal or upon the death of the president, the vice president takes office. If the vice president is also removed from office, or dies, the Speaker of the House of Representatives would take office as president of the United States.

The third branch of the federal government is the judicial branch. Its function is to interpret the laws. To do this, there is a network of federal courts, the highest of which is the Supreme Court.

Briefly, this explains the **separation of powers.** Now let us see how the **system of checks and balances** works.

Each of the three branches of government has been set up to check the other branches. For example, the president must sign into law all bills passed by Congress; if he thinks that a bill is not good, he can veto or say no to that bill. Then the bill must go back to Congress. It can only be passed by a two-thirds vote of both houses of Congress after the president's veto.

The president appoints many high government officials, his cabinet, head of agencies, and federal judges (even those of the Supreme Court). But all of these appointments must be approved by the Senate. This is one way the legislative branch checks the executive branch.

In this process, the judicial branch has the "last word" over the other two branches. The Supreme Court may decide that a law made by Congress and signed by the president is unconstitutional; that is, it is not in accordance with the Constitution. There is no appeal from a decision of the Supreme Court!

REVIEW

Do you know what these words mean? Write the meaning next to the word. If you are not sure, look up the meaning in the Word List at the end of the book.

1. judicial _____

2. interpret _____

3. Senate _____

4. House of Representatives _____

5. separation of powers _____

6. system of checks and balances_____

7. legislative_____

8. executive_____

From the list of new words in items 1–8, choose the words that fit in the blanks in sentences 9–13.

9. Two principles on which our government is based are_____

   and _____.

10. The _____ branch is made up of two houses,

    the _____ and the _____.

11. The _____ branch carries out the laws.

12. If the president dies or is unable to perform his duties, the _____

    _____ becomes president.

13. The _____ branch, made up of a series of courts,

    _____ the law.

See the answer key on page 212.

Congress: Your Representatives

The legislative branch of the federal government is called the **Congress,** which, according to the Constitution, has power to make laws for the nation. The Constitution also sets the qualifications for senators and representatives and tells how they are to be elected.

At the present time, there are **100 senators (two from each of the 50 states) and 435 representatives apportioned according to population.** In the Senate both of the senators from your state represent you, but in the House of Representatives only the representative from the district where you live represents you.

The function of Congress is to make laws, but nowhere in the Constitution is there a statement of the exact steps that must be taken in the law-making process. The steps by which a bill introduced by a senator or a representative becomes a law have developed over the years. In fact, the whole committee system, so important in the law-making process, was set up by Congress in order to handle its business more efficiently.

A Tripartite System

The Principle of Checks and Balances in our Government

(Examples are shown below)

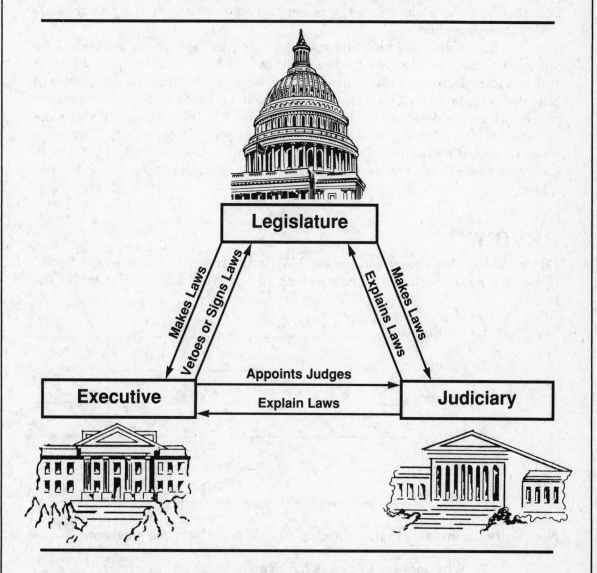

This chart indicates one way in which each branch of our Federal Government is authorized to check (to hold back, to slow up, and even to change) the action of each of the other two branches.

Figure 19

Source: U.S. Department of Justice, Immigration and Naturalization Service

Congress begins its sessions on January 3 of each year and is in session until the members of both Houses vote to **adjourn,** or close, the meeting. Each of the Houses has its own chairperson: The vice president presides over the Senate; the speaker of the House of Representatives is chosen by the members of that body and presides over all of its sessions.

Congress has many important powers: to coin money, to set taxes and collect them, to declare war, and (a very important power to you) to establish the requirements for naturalization. It has many other powers, and each of the Houses has some special powers: for example, all bills relating to money must be proposed in the House of Representatives and passed there before going to the Senate. The Senate alone has the power to **ratify,** or approve, a treaty made with a foreign country.

Sometimes you hear the word *bill* used to describe an act being considered by Congress. Do you know the difference between a bill and a law? A **bill** is a formal proposal recommended by a member of Congress. Thousands of bills are introduced in Congress each year, but many do not become laws because, after consideration by committees or by the full House, they are not approved. Even after a bill is approved by a majority vote in both Houses, it must be signed by the president. If the president vetoes the bill, it returns to Congress where it must be passed by a two-thirds vote. Only then does it become a **law!**

REVIEW

Do you know what these words mean? Write the meanings next to the words. If you are not sure, look up the meaning in the Word List at the end of the book.

1. qualification _____

2. apportion_____

3. adjourn _____

4. ratify _____

5. treaty _____

6. majority_____

Now, write the answers to the following questions in the space provided.

7. Why does the Congress have two houses?_____

   _____

8. Can you introduce a bill in Congress? _____

   _____

9. When does Congress begin each session? _____

   _____

HOW A BILL BECOMES A LAW

1. Bill introduced in the House of Representatives

Bill is pigeon-holed by committee, and forced out of committee by a majority vote of the House

OR

THEN

2. To committee for study and possible public hearings; bill may be amended, or rewritten, or passed without any changes

3. To whole House for debate; may be amended and passed, or passed by whole House without amendment

4. To Senate for action

5. To Senate committee for study; passed by Senate committee

Bill amended and passed by Senate

THEN

OR

6. Debated in Senate and passed by whole Senate

To conference of members of both Houses; conference members agree, and whole House and whole Senate accept conference bill

THEN

7. To President for signature

8. President signs bill and it becomes law

Figure 20

Source: U.S. Department of Justice, Immigration and Naturalization Service

Executive Branch of Our Federal Government

The Executive Branch Enforces the Laws

1—The President
Qualifications:
    (1) Natural-born citizen of the
        United States.
    (2) At least thirty-five years of
        age when taking office.
    (3) At least fourteen years a
        resident of the United States.

2—The Vice President
Qualifications:
The same as required for
the President.

3—The Cabinet Members
Qualifications:
None expressed in the law.

Duties:
To advise the President and
to manage their respective
agencies properly.

Figure 21

Source: U.S. Department of Justice, Immigration and Naturalization Service

The President

Term of office—4 years.
Salary—$200,000 a year.
Election—November of every fourth year.
Inauguration—January 20 following election.
Elected—By the people through the Electoral College.
Qualifications—Natural-born citizen at least 35 years old and at least 14 years a resident of the United States.

Succession to the office—(People next in line to be president if the president cannot carry out his or her duties.)
1. Vice President.
2. Speaker of the House of Representatives.
3. President <u>pro tempore</u> of the Senate.
4. Secretary of State.
5. Secretary of the Treasury.
6. Secretary of Defense.
7. Attorney General.
8. Secretary of the Interior.
9. Secretary of Agriculture.
10. Secretary of Commerce.
11. Secretary of Labor.
12. Secretary of Health and Human Services.
13. Secretary of Housing and Urban Development.
14. Secretary of Transportation.
15. Secretary of Energy.
16. Secretary of Education.
17. Secretary of Veterans' Affairs.

Chief power and duty—To enforce the Constitution, the laws made by the Congress, and treaties.

Other powers—
1. To veto bills.
2. To recommend bills to the Congress.
3. To call special sessions of the Congress.
4. To deliver messages to the Congress.
5. To appoint Federal judges.
6. To appoint representatives to foreign countries.
7. To appoint Department heads and other important officials.
8. To pardon.
9. To carry on official business with foreign nations.
10. To be Commander-in-Chief of the Armed Forces.

<u>Figure 22</u>

Source: U.S. Department of Justice, Immigration and Naturalization Service

10. When does Congress adjourn? _____

_____

11. How does a bill become a law? _____

_____

Note the following paragraph.

An English writer once said that the men who founded the United States had a clear idea of what they wanted to put into the Constitution and then left it to later generations to work out the details. He added that this plan has been remarkably successful.

12. In your own words, write one example of this.

_____

_____

_____

See the answer key on page 212.

The Presidency

The president is the **chief executive,** or head, of the federal government. His job is to carry out the laws and to manage the affairs of the country. Only the president and the vice president can be voted for by all the citizens of the United States. Both are elected for terms of four years and cannot serve for more than two terms, as provided in Amendment 22 of the Constitution.

The president and his family live in the White House, at 1600 Pennsylvania Avenue, Washington, D.C., a building that symbolizes the dignity of the office. The president also has his office here. If you write a letter to the president, you should address him as Mr. President.

The president takes the oath of office on January 20 following his election. Just as your Oath of Allegiance will be administered by a judge when you become a citizen, the president's oath is administered by a judge—the highest ranking judge in the country, the **Chief Justice of the Supreme Court.**

Here is the oath that the president takes.

PRESIDENTIAL OATH OF OFFICE

I do solemnly swear that I will faithfully execute the office of President of the United States, and will to the best of my ability, preserve, protect and defend the Constitution of the United States.

Because the president has many important responsibilities, he appoints people to help him. These people, each heading an executive department, make up the cabinet. There are 14 departments in the cabinet. All cabinet members must be approved by the Senate before they can serve. Remember, this is part of our system of checks and balances! Following are the cabinet members and their duties:

Position	Duties
Attorney General	heads the Department of Justice (including the Immigration and Naturalization Service) and represents the government in all legal matters.
Secretary of Agriculture	manages farming and the improvement of conditions among farmers.
Secretary of Commerce	manages trade relations between the U.S. and other countries and helps business people.
Secretary of Defense	manages the armed services (Army, Navy, Air Force, and Marines).
Secretary of Education	supervises special programs of education authorized by the Congress.
Secretary of Energy	coordinates the work of agencies relating to the development of power.
Secretary of Health and Human Services	is in charge of the common needs of the people, including social security, child labor, and public health and assistance.
Secretary of Housing and Urban Development	handles the financing and construction of public housing.
Secretary of the Interior	takes care of all public lands.
Secretary of Labor	manages the conditions of working people.
Secretary of State	has charge of all foreign affairs.
Secretary of Transportation	coordinates different kinds of transportation: aviation, highways, railroads, and so on.
Secretary of the Treasury	has charge of federal funds and taxes.
Secretary of Veterans' Affairs	oversees programs and advises president.

Now you know what heavy responsibilities may rest with the president and his advisers (the cabinet).

What about the vice president? As you may remember, he presides over the Senate at all of its sessions. That is an important responsibility. But probably the vice president's most important duty is to become president if the president dies, resigns, or is removed from office.

The first president of the United States was George Washington. His birthday, in February, is a national holiday. George Washington commanded the army during the American Revolution and brought a group of inexperienced, poorly equipped soldiers to victory. When the Constitution was written, it provided that one of the duties of the president was to be commander-in-chief of the armed forces.

Another president whose birthday is a holiday, at least in some parts of the country, is Abraham Lincoln, who served during the Civil War and who is credited with saving the Union and freeing the slaves with the Emancipation Proclamation.

REVIEW

Do you know what these words mean? Write the meanings next to the words. If you are not sure, look up the meaning in the Word List at the end of the book.

1. chief executive _____

2. oath _____

3. commerce _____

4. energy _____

5. treasury _____

6. cabinet _____

7. agriculture _____

8. urban _____

9. attorney _____

Now write the answers to the following questions in the space provided.

10. Is the president's most important duty to make the laws or to carry them out? _____

_____

11. Does the president have many responsibilities or a few responsibilities? _____

_____

12. Who helps the president? _____

_____

13. Can a naturalized citizen become president of the United States?

_____

14. What oath does the president take? When does he take it? _____

_____

See the answer key on page 212.

The Court System

The **judicial branch** of the government is responsible for interpreting the laws. The Constitution calls for one Supreme Court and "such inferior [lower] courts as the Congress shall from time to time ordain and establish."

Judicial Branch of Our Federal Government
The Courts Explain the Laws

The Supreme Court is the Highest Court in the Land

Regular Courts

One Supreme Court

Courts of Appeals in the 11 Circuits

94 District Courts

Special Courts

One Court of Claims (1855)	One Court of Customs (1926)	One Court of Customs and Patent Appeals	Court of Military Appeals

"Equal Justice Under Law"

Figure 23

Source: U.S. Department of Justice, Immigration and Naturalization Service

Congress has set up a series of lower federal courts that have the right to hear and decide cases under federal laws. This system of courts includes district courts, courts of appeal, and finally the **Supreme Court,** the highest court of the country. Once the Supreme Court has made a decision, that is the last word. There can be no further appeal.

There are nine judges on the Supreme Court, all appointed by the president for life. When a case comes before the Supreme Court, the justices hear it together. The decision is reached by majority vote. Sometimes, justices who disagree, or **dissent,** write minority or dissenting opinions. But the majority vote is final.

At one time, the Supreme Court justices were referred to as the "nine old men" but that is no longer appropriate, since in 1981 the first woman justice was appointed to the Supreme Court.

The lower federal courts have jurisdiction, or authority, in disputes over government security, immigration, national banks, shipping on the high seas, and other matters. Cases that most of us are involved in are decided at the state or local level. Each state has a network of courts in which persons who have broken state laws are tried. Each city also has courts in which cases involving local laws are tried.

REVIEW

Do you know what these words mean? Write the meanings next to the words. If you are not sure, look up the meaning in the Word List at the end of the book.

1. appeal _____

2. dispute_____

3. jurisdiction _____

4. dissent (dissenting)_____

Now, write the answers to the following questions in the space provided.

5. What is the function of the judicial branch of the government? ___

_____

6. What is the highest court in the United States?_____

_____

7. How is this court set up?_____

_____

8. Who is presently the chief justice? _____

_____

9. Are there any courts other than federal courts? _____

_____

Match the first part of each sentence (column A) with the letter in column B in order to make a complete thought. (Choices may be repeated.)

COLUMN A	COLUMN B
10. _____ Disputes under federal laws	a. that a law is unconstitutional.
11. _____ Naturalization procedures	b. related to shipping on the high sea.
12. _____ The Supreme Court can decide	c. are handled by federal courts.
13. _____ Violations of local law	d. are handled by local courts.

See the answer key on page 212.

State and Local Governments

State Government

When you apply for naturalization, you must prove that you have lived for at least three months in the state from which you apply. You should know the names of the governor and the two senators from your state.

Each of the 50 states has three branches of government—legislative, executive, judicial—just like the U.S. federal government, but not all of them function in the same way. The reason that different patterns emerged is because the 13 original colonies had governments before the U.S. Constitution was ratified in 1789. The first to have its own constitution was New Hampshire. In fact, if you visit New Hampshire today, you will see the nation's oldest state legislature still functioning in its original chambers.

Like Congress, the state legislatures make laws for the state, but they cannot make laws that affect all Americans. They cannot declare war, regulate post offices, coin money, control trade with foreign countries, or decide who can become American citizens. According to the U.S. Constitution (the Tenth Amendment), the states have those powers that are not granted to the federal government and that are not specifically denied to them. This gives the states a great deal of power over our everyday lives. Education, health, sanitation, police and fire protection, and voting procedures are some examples of state functions. States impose taxes, even income taxes, regulate businesses that operate within their borders, and perform many functions that protect the lives and property of their residents.

Each state has a chief executive, or governor, elected by the people of the state, who makes sure that the laws are carried out. Like the president, the governor has people to assist and advise him.

The judicial branch of state governments includes a set of courts that have authority to try civil and criminal cases; some states have family and children's courts. All have courts of appeal. All states have correctional departments that regulate jails and prisons within their jurisdiction.

Local Government

Within the states there are smaller subdivisions—counties, cities, towns, and villages—that have governments, too. Laws for their residents are made by bodies often called councils, which have the authority to control streets, traffic, water supply, garbage, parking, and other everyday services. Cities and counties may also impose taxes, such as property and school taxes.

This government has an executive branch too, sometimes headed by a mayor or commissioner, which sees that local laws are enforced. And there is a judicial branch, consisting of municipal courts, traffic courts, and, in some cases, small claims courts. Local governments vary most from state to state. Find out how your local government functions, and when you become a citizen, get involved at this level! It is at this level that residents are in closest contact with their elected officials.

As you learn more about what state and local governments can do, remember that the U.S. Constitution is the supreme law of the land and the Supreme Court can find laws unconstitutional if they go against the Constitution.

REVIEW

Do you know what these words mean? Write the meanings next to the words. If you are not sure, look up the meaning in the Word List at the end of the book.

1. function _____

2. executive _____

3. ratified _____

4. legislative _____

5. legislature _____

6. judicial _____

7. jurisdiction _____

8. unconstitutional _____

Now, write the answers to the following question in the space provided.

9. How does the U.S. Constitution grant rights to the 50 states? _____

_____

HOW THE ORGANIZATION OF GOVERNMENT IN CITIES, STATES, AND THE NATION IS MUCH ALIKE

	Each has a Legislative Branch to make laws	Each has an Executive Branch to enforce the laws	Each has a Judicial Branch to explain and apply the laws
The Federal Government:	The Congress. —Senate and House of Representatives.	President, Vice President, 11 Executive Departments, and other executive agencies.	The Federal courts.
The State Government:	The State Legislature. (Two houses in all States but Nebraska.)	The governor and heads of executive departments.	The State courts.
The City Government:	The City Council or Commissioners.	The mayor or manager or board of commissioners.	The city courts.

Figure 24

Source: U.S. Department of Justice, Immigration and Naturalization Service.

DELEGATED POWERS IN THE FEDERAL SYSTEM

A. POWERS OF THE FEDERAL GOVERNMENT
(those DELEGATED to it)

EXAMPLES

To control relations with foreign nations.

To punish crimes against the United States.

To establish post offices.

To coin money and regulate its value.

To keep up an army, a navy, and an air corps.

To declare war and make peace.

To set standards for weights and measures.

To regulate commerce among the States and with foreign countries.

To make <u>uniform</u> laws about naturalization and <u>bankruptcy</u>.

To protect authors and inventors by giving <u>copyrights</u> and patents.

To admit new States and to control the territory of the United States.

To make all laws necessary and proper for carrying into effect the expressly stated powers and all othe powers granted by the United States Constitution.

B. CONCURRENT POWERS*

EXAMPLES

To borrow money.

To collect taxes.

To build public works.

To charter banks.

To establish courts.

To help agriculture and industry.

To protect the public health.

C. PROHIBITED POWERS

EXAMPLES

To deny <u>civil rights</u> (such as freedom of speech, press, religion, and assembly).

To pass laws that make illegal something that has already been done legally and honestly.

To pass a law that finds any person guilty without trial.

D. POWERS OF THE STATES (called RESERVED powers)

EXAMPLES

To authorize the establishment of local governments.

To establish and keep up schools.

To regulate city government groups.

To provide for a State militia.

To regulate commerce within the borders of the State.

To regulate labor, industry, and business within the State.

To provide care for <u>orphans</u> and paupers, and for blind, crippled, insane, and other helpless persons.

To make laws on all other subjects not prohibited to the States by the Federal or State Constitutions, and not delegated to the Federal Government.

*Concurrent means belonging to both federal and state governments.

Figure 25

Source: U.S. Department of Justice, Immigration and Naturalization Service

The Federal System

The People of the United States have provided

through

The Federal Constitution

That Certain Powers of Government be

Delegated to the Federal Government	Shared by both the Federal and State Governments	Reserved to the State Governments

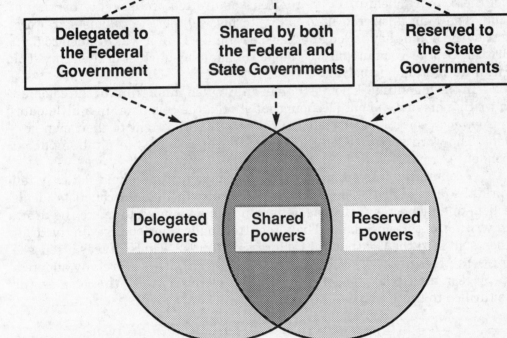

Delegated Powers | **Shared Powers** | **Reserved Powers**

"The powers not delegated to the United States by the Constitution nor *prohibited* by it to the states are reserved to the states respectively, or to the people." The 10th Amendment of the Constitution of the United States.

Figure 26

Source: U.S. Department of Justice, Immigration and Naturalization Service

The Declaration of Independence

The Fourth of July (**Independence Day**) is the most important of our holidays. It celebrates the birth of a new nation, the United States of America, on July 4, 1776. On that date the United States announced its final separation from Great Britain and told the world that it was a free and independent country. Before this, there had always been the thought that if the British changed their treatment of the colonies, the colonists might be willing to return as part of that country. The ties to Britain were strong, but the Declaration of Independence changed all that! Let us see what happened.

By 1773, there were 13 colonies under British rule, which, at first, was quite liberal. Gradually, more and more laws were made that were harsh and unjust to the colonies. The tax laws were especially unfair. "No Taxation without Representation" became a slogan to express the colonists' dissatisfaction with having to pay taxes they had not voted for. Of course, the colonies had no voice in the British government, and this was a cause of further dissatisfaction.

The colonists finally decided to take action. At a meeting of representatives of the colonies, held in 1774, a letter was drafted and sent to the king of England. The king answered it in angry terms, calling the colonists traitors. This upset them and they called another meeting. In 1775 it was decided to fight the British. George Washington was made commander-in-chief of the army. The American Revolution had begun.

In the meantime, Thomas Paine, an English immigrant to the colonies, began writing his ideas about freedom that stirred the colonists. In a little pamphlet, *Common Sense,* he said that the colonies had the right to their own government. The word spread. Soon the leaders of the colonies were talking about independence.

A committee was set up to write a document that would not only tell the world the facts of British injustice but would also include the colonists' ideals of freedom and democracy. Thomas Jefferson was appointed to make the draft, or first writing, of this document. The committee made some changes in the draft and then sent it to the Continental Congress on June 2. There, it was discussed by representatives of the 13 colonies. On July 4, 1776, it was formally adopted. When copies of the Declaration of Independence were sent to all the colonies, the people thrilled to these words.

> *We hold these truths to be self-evident, that all men are created equal, that they are endowed by their Creator with certain unalienable rights, that among these are life, liberty, and the pursuit of happiness. . .*

The whole declaration appears in the Appendix of this book. Briefly, the declaration states that governments are set up to protect the rights of the people and that laws can be made only when the people agree to them. That is the basis of democracy.

REVIEW

Do you know what these words mean? Write the meanings next to the words. If you are not sure, look up the meaning in the Word List at the end of the book.

1. traitor _____

2. unalienable _____

3. dissatisfaction _____

4. representation _____

5. slogan _____

6. democracy _____

Now write the answers to the following questions in the blanks provided.

7. No taxation without _____ was a popular slogan in the colonies.

8. Rights that belong to us and can never be taken away are____ _____ rights.

9. _____ has been called a government of the people, by the people, and for the people.

10. The king of England called the colonists _____; a_____ is an enemy of the country.

11. By writing to the king, the colonists expressed their _____ with the treatment they had received from the British.

See the answer key on page 212.

THE LIBERTY BELL
"Let Freedom Ring"

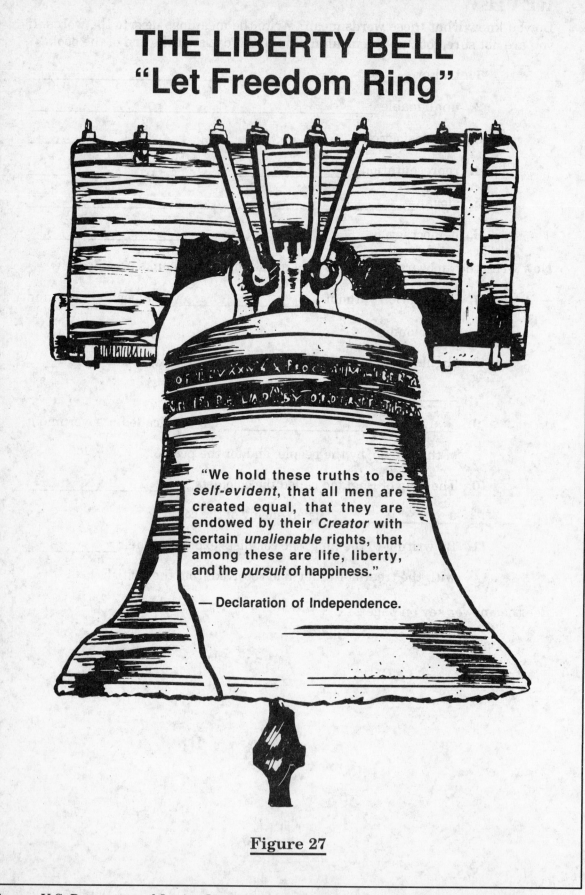

"We hold these truths to be *self-evident*, that all men are created equal, that they are endowed by their *Creator* with certain *unalienable* rights, that among these are life, liberty, and the *pursuit* of happiness."

— Declaration of Independence.

Figure 27

Source: U.S. Department of Justice, Immigration and Naturalization Service

The American Flag

The **flag** is a symbol of our country. The colors of the flag have special meanings: RED is for courage; WHITE is for truth; BLUE is for honor. The American national **anthem** is the **"Star-Spangled Banner,"** which refers to the flag. Sometimes the flag is called other names—Old Glory, the Stars and Stripes, the Red, White, and Blue, or just the Colors. Before the American Revolution, most of the colonies used the British flag. But when anger grew at their treatment by Great Britain, the colonists took down that flag and put up their own.

One year after the Declaration of Independence, in 1777, the American flag was officially adopted. It was made by Betsy Ross. The first flag had 13 stripes, to mark the colonies, and 13 stars, to mark the 13 states. There are still the same number of stripes as in 1777; the number of stars, however, has changed as new states joined the union. The flag that was flown on the moon when the American astronauts landed there in 1969 had 50 stars and 13 stripes. It is the same today. Flag Day is June 14, for it was on that day in 1777 that the first American flag was adopted.

Have you gone to any public meetings where the Pledge of Allegiance was said? You will remember that people stood up and placed their right hands over their hearts as they said these words:

PLEDGE OF ALLEGIANCE

I pledge allegiance to the flag of the United States of America and to the Republic for which it stands: One nation under God, indivisible, with liberty and justice for all.

Where did you hear the word *allegiance* before? That's right! In the final step in the naturalization process, before becoming an American citizen, you must take the Oath of Allegiance. Let's read it.

OATH OF ALLEGIANCE

I hereby declare, on oath, that I absolutely and entirely renounce and abjure all allegiance and fidelity to any foreign prince, potentate, state or sovereignty of whom or which I have heretofore been a subject or a citizen; that I will support and defend the Constitution and laws of the United States of America against all enemies, foreign and domestic; that I will bear true faith and allegiance to the same; that I will bear arms on behalf of the United States or perform noncombatant service in the Armed Forces of the United States when required by law; and that I take this obligation freely without any mental reservation or purpose of evasion, so help me God.

REVIEW

Do you know what these words mean? Write the meanings next to the words. If you are not sure, look up the meaning in the Word List at the end of the book.

1. symbol _____

2. anthem _____

3. "Star-Spangled Banner" _____

4. adopt _____

5. Pledge of Allegiance _____

Now, complete the following sentences in the space provided by adding the word *because* and giving a reason.

Example: We show respect to the flag *because it is the symbol of our country.*

6. The flag is sometimes called the Red, White, and Blue _____

_____

7. The flag has 13 stripes_____

_____

8. It has 50 stars _____

_____

9. Before the American Revolution, most of the colonies used the

British flag _____

10. June 14 is celebrated as Flag Day _____

_____

See the answer key on page 212.

DISPLAYING THE FLAG

Here are two things that we should know about the use of the American flag:

1. When we display the American flag with other flags, our flag should always have the place of honor.

2. The American flag should not be used in advertising (sales, and so on).

108
You Are Ready!

Before You Go On to the Final Test:

Review the Steps to Citizenship.

1. Check your eligibility.
2. Send away for the Application for Naturalization and other forms you may need.
3. Become familiar with the requirements for naturalization—both personal and educational.
4. Fill out the forms, file them, and pay the appropriate fees.
5. Practice the answers to important questions.
6. Be able to express yourself in simple English by practicing your reading, writing, and speaking skills.

The Final Test

Test yourself by answering the questions in the space provided. If you get several questions wrong, be sure to review Step 4 again. Even if you do well, be sure to review the reference materials in the Appendix.

1. Who is credited with discovering America? When?_____

   _____

2. When was the first permanent settlement in America established?

   Where?_____

   _____

3. Who landed at Plymouth Rock in 1620? _____

   _____

4. From what country did we become independent? _____

   _____

5. What is taxation without representation? _____

   _____

6. When was the Declaration of Independence adopted?_____

   _____

7. When was our country first called "The United States of

   America"? _____

   _____

8. Who was the first president of the United States of America? _____

_____

9. Who was Abraham Lincoln? _____

_____

10. What was the Emancipation Proclamation? _____

_____

11. What kind of government does the United States have? _____

_____

12. What is the supreme law of the land? _____

_____

13. When was it adopted? _____

_____

14 . Has it ever been changed? _____

_____

15. What are the branches of the federal government? _____

_____

16. Who makes the laws for the United States? _____

_____

17. What is the highest court in the United States? _____

_____

18. Are there other governments besides the federal government?
    What are they? _____

_____

19. How many states are there in the United States? _____

_____

20. What are the colors of the American flag? What do they stand for?

_____

21. What is the name of the national anthem? _____

_____

22. Who was president during the Civil War? _____

_____

23. If a law is declared unconstitutional by the Supreme Court, what

happens to it?_____

_____

24. If the president does not approve a bill sent to him by Congress,

what can he do? _____

_____

25. Can the bill still become a law?_____

_____

Check your answers to these questions with the Answer Key on page 213.

Some Personal Questions

Who is the governor of the state where you live? _____

_____

Who is the mayor, or head, of the local government?_____

_____

Why did you want to come to the United States? _____

_____

Why do you want to become a citizen?_____

_____

Check your answers with a friend.

Step 5—The Naturalization Interview and the Oath

Some time after you file your N-400, Application for Naturalization, you will be called for the interview. You will receive a letter telling you when and where to appear. *A naturalization examiner will question you about your knowledge of American history and government (civics). The examiner will also observe whether you speak, read, and write English well enough to become a citizen.* (Persons over 50 years of age who have lived in the United States as permanent residents for over 20 years or over 55 years of age with 15 years of residence are excused from the English requirement. And disabled persons may be exempt from both the English and civics requirements.) It is not necessary to have any friends or relatives with you at this time.

After the interview and the approval of your application for naturalization, you will be notified of the time and place of your naturalization ceremony, where you will take the Oath of Allegiance to the United States. There is no exact date for the ceremony. In some cases, you may have the option of taking the Oath on the same day as your interview. In other cases, you may wait anywhere from 2 weeks to 6 months. After you take the Oath, you will receive your Certificate of Naturalization as a new citizen of the United States!

Be on time—or a few minutes early—for each appointment. Dress carefully and neatly, as though you were going to a job interview. Remember to bring your Permanent Resident Card with you. And don't be nervous! Naturalization examiners know how you feel about this big step. They are understanding people. If you are prepared, you have nothing to worry about.

One Applicant's Report

That day finally arrived! The notice had given Ann the date, time, and place for her citizenship interview. She had marked her calendar, assembled all her papers, and selected her navy blue suit for the occasion. And now that day had arrived. Ann left the house early enough to arrive at 26 Federal Plaza 15 minutes before the time scheduled for her interview. To be safe, she had the originals and copies of all her papers, her passport, birth certificate, marriage certificate, and death certificate for her late husband. She had also copies of the income tax forms she had filed. She put them all in a big envelope.

She arrived at 26 Federal Plaza 15 minutes before the appointed time. When there, a court officer asked her to raise her right hand and to swear to tell the truth, and nothing but the truth. She did so. That was easy. And the interview began with personal questions such as "What is your address, telephone number, and social security number?" And then some others about her job, her family, whether she had been on public assistance, or had used drugs. She answered them all quickly. One question that she had to look up in her notes was the name of any club or organization she had belonged to in her country of birth. She could easily report the club she had joined since coming to the United States— the Parent-Teachers Association of her daughter's school. The interviewer seemed pleased with her answers. She was then asked questions to determine her knowledge of American history and government.

Some of those questions that she recalled were: What are the colors of the American flag, and what do they represent? What is the capital of the United States? Who is the President? Who was the first President? Who was the President during the Civil War? What is Independence Day, and why do we celebrate it? Who is the Governor of New York State, and who is the Mayor of New York City? How many states are there? She was also asked to name two states other than New York and New Jersey. Then she had to write a few sentences that the interviewer dictated. She recalled she was asked to write a little about why she wanted to become a citizen. That was easy.

OATH OF ALLEGIANCE

I hereby declare, on oath, that I absolutely and entirely renounce and abjure all allegiance and fidelity to any foreign prince, potentate, state or sovereignty of whom or which I have heretofore been a subject or a citizen; that I will support and defend the Constitution and laws of the United States of America against all enemies, foreign and domestic; that I will bear true faith and allegiance to the same; that I will bear arms on behalf of the United States or perform noncombatant service in the Armed Forces of the United States when required by law; and that I take this obligation freely without any mental reservation or purpose of evasion, so help me God.

Review of the Steps to Citizenship

Print your name here _____

Your address here _____

_____

_____

The date here _____(month first)

The name of the current president of the United States is _____

The two senators from my state are _____

and_____.

I live in the_____Congressional District. The name of my

representative is_____.

Now go back to Part One to check your answers. How did you do?

Before you go on to the next unit, answer these questions:

- Have you filled in the sample forms in this book?
- Have you filled in your own Application for Naturalization and other forms you may need?
- Have you filed these forms and paid the required fees?

If you answered "yes" to these three questions, you are on your way to success.

Review of the Probability Questions

These are the same 25 questions that we called probability questions in Step 2, but here they have been rephrased in the way your interviewer may ask them. Do not look back at the ones in Step 2 until you have finished these.

1. How many states are in the United States of America? _____

    _____

2. What are the colors of the flag? _____

3. How many stars are there on our flag? _____

4. What do the stars stand for? _____

5. How many stripes are there? _____

6. What do the stripes stand for?_____

7. What is the Fourth of July? _____

8. Who was the first president of the United States of America?_____

    _____

9. Who is president today? _____

10. Who is the vice president? _____

11. What is the Constitution?_____

12. Can the Constitution be changed? If so, what are the changes

    called? _____

13. How many branches are in the government?_____

14. What are these branches of our government? _____

15. Which branch makes the laws?_____

16. Which branch carries out the laws? _____

17. Which branch sees to it that all laws are in accordance with the

    Constitution? _____

18. What is the highest court in our land? _____

19. What is the Bill of Rights? _____

20. What is the Fourteenth Amendment to the Constitution? _____

_____

21. What are the two houses of Congress?_____

22. Can you name the persons who represent you in Congress? _____

_____

23. Who was Abraham Lincoln? _____

24. What other governments besides the federal government are there? _____

25. What is the Supreme Court? _____

Now look at the answers under Probability Questions on pages 64–66.

APPENDIX
★★★★★★★★★★★★★★★★★★★★★★★★
For Ready Reference

American English:
Idiomatic Expressions

American English:
Pronunciation Practice

National Holidays

Special Observances

The Declaration of
Independence

The Constitution

A Look at American History

Immigration Update

Sample Completed Form
N-400

Word List

Answer Key

American English: Idiomatic Expressions

The American language and customs often are difficult for students. Many teachers find that their pupils encounter unnecessary difficulty with the examination for naturalization. This section provides specific American English language practice and orientation.

The non-English speaker in the United States, or the newcomer of limited educational background, has difficulty facing differences in language and culture, especially within the context of the naturalization examinations. Everybody has the same problem. Even if you have overcome the basic differences and are on your way to fluency in the new language, you will be helped by the step-by-step presentation in this guide.

For the most part, the naturalization examination is an oral test. The examiner asks the questions; you answer them. Your answer depends on how you interpret the question. If the examiner uses expressions you don't understand, you may be *at a loss!* You can see how important it is to become familiar with different patterns of American speech and with a wide range of special expressions that Americans use as part of their everyday lives. When you practice using these expressions yourself, you will become more confident and successful in your own everyday exchanges with natural-born Americans. Success breeds success! Does that *ring a bell* with you? Of course! *It figures* that this new fluency will help you reach one more step *up the ladder* of success to community participation and, eventually, to real citizenship.

Idioms are groups of words used together in a special sense. They are expressions regularly used in that certain way. There are four examples in what you have just read. The meanings are easy. Say them now—say the entire sentence out loud. Then repeat only the idioms. That's it!

Another example that may help before you study the lists comes from my own experience as a teacher of English.

One day, one of my students raised his hand to ask, "What is a teasy?"

"Do you mean a tease?" I asked.

"Not a tease! A teasy, I hear it all the time. In the subway, many people push and shove. Then some people say, "Take a Teasy!"

I explained the meaning of *take it easy*. And my student was happy. *Take it easy* is a common American expression.

Of course, you know that it means to relax, slow down. Another idiom like it is *easy does it*. Say them both now. Make them part of your language!

More Common Idioms

Word	Idiom	Meaning
according	according to	— on the authority
all	all right	— satisfactory
	all at once, all of a sudden	— unexpectedly
	all day (night, week, month)	— continuously
along	go along with	— agree (with an idea)
	get along with	— agree (with a person)
as	as a matter of fact	— really
	as soon as	— when
at	at all (not at all)	— to any degree
be	be over	— finished
bear	bear in mind (keep in mind)	— remember
break	break down	— fall apart
	breakdown	— failure to function
by	by heart	— by memory
	by myself	— alone
	by the way	— incidentally
call	call on	— request help from, visit
	call up	— telephone
catch	catch cold	— get a cold
	catch fire	— get on fire, burn
change	change of $10	— money
	change one's mind	— decide differently
charge	in charge of	— be responsible for
	be charged with (robbery, murder, etc.)	— having a statement made against
count	count on	— depend
cover	to cover up	— to hide something,
	cover up	something concealed
cross	to cross the street	— to go across
	to cross out	— to draw a line through
day	day off	— nonworking day
	day in, day out	— all the time

Word	Idiom	Meaning
do	to do one's best	— to try hard
	what do you *do?*	— what is your work?
		(answer: *I'm a* lawyer, plumber, etc.)
	do over	— to correct
else	what else, where else	— besides the answer given
entitled	to be entitled to	— to deserve (by law)
every	every now and then	— from time to time
	every other day	— on two days with a day in between
figure out	can you figure out the meaning?	— estimate, determine
file	to file a claim, a report, document	— to turn over a paper to the proper authority
fill	fill in (the form, etc.), fill out	— to put in what is necessary
find	to find out	— to learn
for	for the present, for the time being	— temporarily
fringe	fringe benefits	— special good things that go with some jobs
get	to get along	— to succeed
	to get along with	— to be friends with
	to get away with	— to escape
	to get in touch with	— to communicate with
going	going to (in the future)	— will go, will do something
had	had better	— it would be a good idea to
hand	hand in	— to submit a paper
	on hand	— in stock
hang	to hang up	— to put back
hear	to hear from	— to get word from
hold	to hold on	— to wait
	to hold off	— to delay
in	in a hurry	— in a rush
	in the long run	— over a long period of time
	in time	— soon enough
just	just a minute	— soon
	just so	— correct
keep	to keep an eye on	— to watch
	to keep in touch with	— to continue communication
	to keep up	— to continue
know	to know by heart	— to memorize
lay	to lay off	— to get let go from a job
little	little by little	— gradually
look	to look after	— to care for
	to look forward to	— to anticipate
	to look into	— to check
	to look up	— to search for

American English: Idiomatic Expressions

Word	Idiom	Meaning
make	to make an appointment	— to set a date for
	to make clear	— to explain
meet	to meet the requirements	— to be eligible
mixed	mixed up	— confused
more	more or less	— for the most part
never	never mind	— forget it
nothing	nothing wrong, nothing the matter	— everything is okay
now	now and then	— once in a while
on	on the radio, television, etc.	— in a program
	on time	— punctual
out	out of order	— not functioning
	out of the question	— not possible
over	do it over and over	— to repeat something many times
pass	pass judgment on	— give an opinion on
	pass a law	— enact a bill
	to pass away	— to die
pick	pick out	— choose
	to pick up	— to take
play	to play ball	— to go along with
point	to point out	— to call attention to
put	to put down	— to suppress
	to put on	— to assume
	to put off	— to postpone
quiet	quiet down	— stop making noise or speaking
quite	quite a few	— many
rather	rather than	— instead of
responsible	responsible for	— in charge of
right	right away	— very soon
say	say the word	— give the order
	to say nothing of	— not to mention
see	to see about	— to check into
	to see to it	— to ensure
take	take an oath	— swear
	take one's time	— go slowly
think	think it over	— consider it carefully
time	to have time	— plenty of time left
up	up-to-date	— timely
used	used to	— in the past
vain	in vain	— without success
very	the very thing	— exactly right

Word	Idiom	Meaning
walk	to walk out	— to leave
while	a little while	— a short time
without	to do without	— to lack
work	to work out	— to exercise
write	to write away for	— to send for

As you can see, English is an idiomatic language. These are only a sample of those you may hear in everyday speech.

REVIEW

As a review, see if you can fill in the blanks in the following sentences with an idiomatic expression from the list.

1. I_____live in Chicago, but now I live in New York.

2. I_____to pay my taxes; they are not due until April.

3. It is_____for me to lend my friend money at this time.

4. Business is so bad, the company will have to_____some workers.

5. Joe worked in a dress factory for_____last year.

6. Please_____for an application for me!

7. Olga is_____to bringing her husband into this country soon.

8. She_____him last week that his application was being checked.

9. "_____, it takes time," said Olga's teacher.

10. "He will have a nervous_____ if he doesn't get his papers soon," she answered.

Check your answer to these questions with the Answer Key on page 213.

American English: Idiomatic Expressions

American English: Pronunciation Practice

Even after many years in their new country, some immigrants still experience difficulties with the *consonant sounds* of American English. If you have problems with Ls, Rs, Bs, Hs, Vs, Th blends, and others, this section is for you.

Practice, practice the positions of the mouth, lips, and tongue, in order to produce the sound correctly. Exaggerate the directions. Use a mirror. In any case, do it every day!

	Say	*Repeat*
Beginning L and R Sounds		
Put tip of tongue	let	Let Lulu do it.
behind upper teeth.	light	Light the lamp.
	right	The answer is right.
	run	Run the race.
T and D, N and S		
Put tip of tongue above	tell	Tell me the time.
upper front teeth.	tight	Too tight.
	don't	Don't run!
	did	Did Dot do her lesson?
	dull	It was too dull.
	no, not	Not at all!
	sunset	The sun sets late in Sweden.

TH
Open lips a little; put
tongue between teeth.

the
this
think

This is the time
to think about supper.

CH, SH, Y, J, and Z
Put middle of tongue
against top of mouth.

chin
ship

join

measure

Place your chin on the ship
   in the bottle.
Charles and John joined the
   union yesterday.
Measure the chair to see if it is
   larger than the old chair.

H Sound
Part your lips and blow.

he
her
home

He asked her to show him
   her new home.

M, P, B, and W (WH) Sounds
Bring your lips together.

Mama
move
Papa
baby
will
what, where

The baby's first word
   was *Papa*, not *Mama*.
What will you do?
Where will you go?

F and V
Bite your lower lip.

fat
very

The very fat man wants
   to be thin.

K, X, G, and NG
Put back of tongue against
top of mouth.

key
exit
girl
sing a song

Keep the exit door locked
   with a key.
The girl keeps singing a
   song all day long.

   This is a simple approach to some sounds that may be difficult for you.
Practice them as often as you can. You will be glad when it is time for your naturalization examination!

National Holidays

You may be asked why we celebrate the national holiday nearest to the time of your naturalization examination. You may wonder why businesses have special sales on February 22. Of course, you know that the Fourth of July/Independence Day is our most important national holiday. Do you know why the following holidays are celebrated nationally?

January 1	New Year's Day
January 15	Birthday of Martin Luther King, Jr.
February 22	Birthday of George Washington
May 30	Memorial Day
July 4	The Fourth of July/Independence Day
First Monday in September	Labor Day
October 12	Columbus Day
November 11	Veterans Day
Fourth Thursday in November	Thanksgiving Day
December 25	Christmas

Some of the days are changed to Monday or Friday, to give people a three-day weekend. And, if the holiday falls on a Sunday, the next day also is celebrated as a holiday.

Special Observances

These are not holidays, but special observances that are held in different parts of the U.S.A.

February 12	Lincoln's Birthday
February 14	St. Valentine's Day
March 17	St. Patrick's Day
Second Sunday in May	Mother's Day
June 14	Flag Day
Third Sunday in June	Father's Day
September 17	Citizenship Day
October 24	United Nations Day
First Tuesday	Election Day
after first Monday in November	

Religious holy dates, of course, also are widely observed.

REVIEW: Holidays and Observances

Read the dates in Column I aloud. Then read Column II. Match the letters with the numbers by drawing lines from one to the other. Lastly, put the letters in the space next to the numbered items. Do it like this:

1. Fourth Thursday   _c_ ——— c. Thanksgiving Day
   in November

	COLUMN I		COLUMN II
1.	October 12	_____	**a.** St. Patrick's Day
2.	December 25	_____	**b.** Labor Day
3.	March 17	_____	**c.** Martin Luther King Jr.'s Birthday
4.	January 15	_____	**d.** Veterans Day
5.	First Monday in September	_____	**e.** Columbus Day
6.	February 22	_____	**f.** Lincoln's Birthday
7.	June 14	_____	**g.** Memorial Day
8.	July 4	_____	**h.** Flag Day
9.	February 12	_____	**i.** George Washington's Birthday
10.	May 30	_____	**j.** Christmas Day
			k. Independence Day

Turn the book upside down to find the right answers.

Answers:
1. e.
2. j.
3. a.
4. c.
5. b.
6. i.
7. h.
8. k.
9. f.
10. g.

The Declaration of Independence

In Congress, July 4, 1776

The Unanimous Declaration of the Thirteen United States of America

When in the course of human events, it becomes necessary for one people to dissolve the political bands which have connected them with another, and to assume among the powers of the earth, the separate and equal station to which the laws of Nature and of Nature's God entitle them, a decent respect to the opinions of mankind requires that they should declare the causes which impel them to the separation.

We hold these truths to be self-evident, that all men are created equal, that they are endowed by their Creator with certain unalienable rights, that among these are life, liberty and the pursuit of happiness. That to secure these rights, governments are instituted among men, deriving their just powers from the consent of the governed,—That whenever any form of government becomes destructive of these ends, it is the right of the people to alter or to abolish it, and to institute new government, laying its foundation on such principles and organizing its powers in such form, as to them shall seem most likely to effect their safety and happiness. Prudence, indeed, will dictate that governments long established should not be changed for light and transient causes; and accordingly all experience hath shown, that mankind are more disposed to suffer, while evils are sufferable, than to right themselves by abolishing the forms to which they are accustomed. But when a long train of abuses and usurpations, pursuing invariably the same object evinces a design to reduce them under absolute despotism, it is their right, it is their duty, to throw off such government, and to provide new guards for their future security.—Such has been the patient sufferance of these colonies; and such is now the necessity which constrains them to alter their former systems of government. The history of the present King of Great Britain is a history of repeated injuries and usurpations, all having in direct object the establishment of an absolute tyranny over these states. To prove this, let facts be submitted to a candid world.

He has refused his assent to laws, the most wholesome and necessary for the public good.

He has forbidden his governors to pass laws of immediate and pressing importance, unless suspended in their operation till his assent should be obtained; and when so suspended, he has utterly neglected to attend to them.

He has refused to pass other laws for the accommodation of large districts of people, unless those people would relinquish the right of representation in the legislature, a right inestimable to them and formidable to tyrants only.

He has called together legislative bodies at places unusual, uncomfortable, and distant from the depository of their public records, for the sole purpose of fatiguing them into compliance with his measures.

He has dissolved Representative Houses repeatedly, for opposing with manly firmness his invasion on the rights of the people.

He has refused for a long time, after such dissolutions, to cause others to be elected; whereby the legislative powers, incapable of annihilation, have returned to the people at large for their exercise; the state remaining in the meantime exposed to all the dangers of invasion from without, and convulsions within.

He has endeavoured to prevent the population of these states; for that purpose obstructing the laws for naturalization of foreigners; refusing to pass others to encourage their migrations hither, and raising the conditions of new appropriations of lands.

133

He has obstructed the administration of justice, by refusing his assent to laws for establishing judiciary powers.

He has made judges dependent on his will alone, for the tenure of their offices, and the amount and payment of their salaries.

He has erected a multitude of new offices, and sent hither swarms of officers to harass our people, and eat out their substance.

He has kept among us, in times of peace, standing armies without the consent of our legislatures.

He has affected to render the military independent of and superior to the civil power.

He has combined with others to subject us to a jurisdiction foreign to our constitution, and unacknowledged by our laws; giving his assent to their acts of pretended legislation:

For quartering large bodies of armed troops among us:

For protecting them, by a mock trial, from punishment for any murders which they should commit on the inhabitants of these states:

For cutting off our trade with all parts of the world:

For imposing taxes on us without our consent:

For depriving us in many cases, of the benefits of trial by jury:

For transporting us beyond seas to be tried for pretended offenses:

For abolishing the free system of English laws in a neighbouring province, establishing therein an arbitrary government, and enlarging its boundaries so as to render it at once an example and fit instrument for introducing the same absolute rule into these colonies:

For taking away our charters, abolishing our most valuable laws, and altering fundamentally the forms of our government.

For suspending our own legislatures, and declaring themselves invested with power to legislate for us in all cases whatsoever. He has abdicated government here, by declaring us out of his protection and waging war against us.

He has plundered our seas, ravaged our coasts, burnt our towns, and destroyed the lives of our people.

He is at this time transporting large armies of foreign mercenaries to complete the works of death, desolation and tyranny, already begun with circumstances of cruelty and perfidy scarcely paralleled in the most barbarous ages and totally unworthy the head of a civilized nation.

He has constrained our fellow citizens taken captive on the high seas to bear arms against their country, to become the executioners of their friends and brethren, or to fall themselves by their hands.

He has excited domestic insurrections amongst us, and has endeavoured to bring on the inhabitants of our frontiers, the merciless Indian savages, whose known rule of warfare is an undistinguished destruction of all ages, sexes, and conditions.

In every stage of these oppressions we have petitioned for redress in the most humble terms: Our repeated petitions have been answered only by repeated injury. A prince, whose character is thus marked by every act which may define a tyrant, is unfit to be the ruler of a free people.

Nor have we been wanting in attentions to our British brethren. We have warned them from time to time of attempts by their legislature to extend an unwarrantable jurisdiction over us. We have reminded them of the circumstances of our emigration and settlement here. We have appealed to their native justice and magnanimity, and we have conjured them by the ties of our common kindred to disavow these usurpations, which, would inevitably interrupt our connections and correspondence. They too have been deaf to the voice of justice and of consanguinity. We must, therefore, acquiesce in the necessary which denounces our separation, and hold them, as we hold the rest of mankind, enemies in war, in peace friends.

WE, THEREFORE the Representatives of the United States of America, in General Congress, Assembled, appealing to the Supreme Judge of the world for the rectitude of our intentions, do, in the name, and by authority of the good people of these colonies, solemnly publish and declare, That these United Colonies are, and of right ought to be FREE AND INDEPENDENT STATES; that they are absolved from all allegiance to the British Crown, and that all political connection between them and the state of Great Britain, is and ought to be totally dissolved; and that as free and independent states, they have full power to levy war, conclude peace, contract alliances, establish commerce, and to do all other acts and things which independent states may of right do. And for the support of this Declaration, with a firm reliance on the protection of Divine Providence, we mutually pledge to each other our lives, our fortunes, and our sacred honor.

JOHN HANCOCK.

New Hampshire

JOSIAH BARTLETT   MATTHEW THORNTON

WM. WHIPPLE

Massachusetts Bay

SAML ADAMS   ROBT TREAT PAINE

JOHN ADAMS   ELBRIDGE GERRY

Rhode Island

STEP. HOPKINS   WILLIAM ELLERY

Connecticut

ROGER SHERMAN   WM. WILLIAMS

SAML HUNTINGTON   OLIVER WOLCOTT

New York

WM. FLOYD   FRANS. LEWIS

PHIL. LIVINGSTON   LEWIS MORRIS

New Jersey

RICHD. STOCKTON   JOHN HART

JNO WITHERSPOON   ABRA CLARK

FRAS. HOPKINSON

Pennsylvania

ROBT MORRIS   JAS. SMITH

BENJAMIN RUSH   GEO. TAYLOR

BENJA. FRANKLIN   JAMES WILSON

JOHN MORTON   GEO. ROSS

GEO. CLYMER

Delaware

CAESAR RODNEY   THO M'KEAN

GEO READ

Maryland

SAMUEL CHASE   CHARLES CARROLL

WM. PACA   of Carrollton

Virginia

GEORGE WYTHE   THOS. NELSON JR.

RICHARD HENRY LEE   FRANCIS LIGHTFOOT LEE

TH JEFFERSON   CARTER BRAXTON

BENJA. HARRISON

North Carolina

WM HOOPER   JOHN PENN

JOSEPH HEWES

South Carolina

EDWARD RUTLEDGE   THOS HEYWARD JUNR.

THOMAS LYNCH JUNR.   ARTHUR MIDDLETON

Georgia

BUTTON GWINNETT   GEO WALTON

LYMAN HALL

The Constitution

Preamble

WE THE PEOPLE of the United States, in order to form a more perfect Union, establish justice, insure domestic tranquility, provide for the common defense, promote the general welfare, and secure the blessings of liberty to ourselves and our posterity, do ordain and establish this Constitution for the United States of America.

Article I

Section 1. All legislative powers herein granted shall be vested in a Congress of the United States, which shall consist of a Senate and House of Representatives.

Section 2. The House of Representatives shall be composed of members chosen every second year by the people of the several states, and the electors in each state shall have the qualifications requisite for electors of the most numerous branch of the state legislature.

No person shall be a Representative who shall not have attained to the age of twenty-five years, and been seven years a citizen of the United States, and who shall not, when elected, be an inhabitant of that state in which he shall be chosen.

Representatives and direct taxes shall be apportioned among the several states which may be included within this Union, according to their respective numbers, which shall be determined by adding to the whole number of free persons, including those bound to service for a term of years, and excluding Indians not taxed, three-fifths of all other persons. The actual enumeration shall be made within three years after the first meeting of the Congress of the United States, and within every subsequent term of ten years, in such manner as they shall by law direct. The number of Representatives shall not exceed one for every thirty thousand, but each state shall have at least one representative; and until such enumeration shall be made, the state of New Hampshire shall be entitled to choose three, Massachusetts eight, Rhode Island and Providence Plantations one, Connecticut five, New York six, New Jersey four, Pennsylvania eight, Delaware one, Maryland six, Virginia ten, North Carolina five, South Carolina five, and Georgia three.

When vacancies happen in the representation from any state, the executive authority thereof shall issue writs of election to fill such vacancies.

The House of Representatives shall choose their Speaker and other officers; and shall have the sole power of impeachment.

Section 3. The Senate of the United States shall be composed of two Senators from each state, chosen by the legislature thereof, for six years and each Senator shall have one vote.

Immediately after they shall be assembled in consequence of the first election, they shall be divided as equally as may be into three classes. The seats of the Senators of the first class shall be vacated at the expiration of the second year, of the second class at the expiration of the fourth year, and of the third class at the expiration of the sixth year so that one-third may be chosen every second year; and if vacancies happen by resignation, or otherwise, during the recess of the legislature of any state, the executive thereof may make temporary appointments until the next meeting of the legislature, which shall then fill such vacancies.

No person shall be a Senator who shall not have attained to the age of thirty years, and been nine years a citizen of the United States, and who shall not, when elected, be an inhabitant of that state for which he shall be chosen.

The Vice President of the United States shall be President of the Senate, but shall have no vote, unless they be equally divided.

The Senate shall choose their other officers, and also a President pro tempore, in the absence of the Vice President, or when he shall exercise the office of President of the United States.

The Senate shall have the sole power to try all impeachments. When sitting for that purpose, they shall be on oath or affirmation. When the President of the United States is tried, the Chief Justice shall preside: And no person shall be convicted without the concurrence of two-thirds of the members present.

Judgment in cases of impeachment shall not extend further than to removal from office, and disqualification to hold and enjoy any office of honor, trust or profit under the United States: but the party convicted shall nevertheless be liable and subject to indictment, trial, judgment and punishment, according to law.

Section 4. The times, places and manner of holding elections for Senators and Representatives, shall be prescribed in each state by the legislature thereof; but the Congress may at any time by law make or alter such regulations, except as to the place of choosing Senators.

The Congress shall assemble at least once in every year, and such meeting shall be on the first Monday in December, unless they shall by law appoint a different day.

Section 5. Each House shall be the judge of the elections, returns and qualifications of its own members, and a majority of each shall constitute a quorum to do business; but a smaller number may adjourn from day to day, and may be authorized to compel the attendance of absent members, in such manner, and under such penalties as each House may provide.

Each House may determine the rules of its proceedings, punish its members for disorderly behaviour, and, with the concurrence of two-thirds, expel a member.

Each House shall keep a journal of its proceedings, and from time to time publish the same, excepting such parts as may in their judgment require secrecy; and the yeas and nays of the members of either House on any question shall, at the desire of one-fifth of those present, be entered on the journal.

Neither House, during the session of Congress, shall, without the consent of the other, adjourn for more than three days, not to any other place than that in which the two Houses shall be sitting.

Section 6. The Senators and Representatives shall receive a compensation for their services, to be ascertained by law, and paid out of the Treasury of the United States. They shall in all cases, except treason, felony and breach of the peace, be privileged from arrest during their attendance at the session of their respective Houses, and in going to and returning from the same; and for any speech or debate in either

House, they shall not be questioned in any other place.

No Senator or Representative shall, during the time for which he was elected, be appointed to any civil office under the authority of the United States, which shall have been created, or the emoluments whereof shall have been increased during such time; and no person holding any office under the United States, shall be a member of either House during his continuance in office.

Section 7. All bills for raising revenue shall originate in the House of Representatives; but the Senate may propose or concur with amendments as on other bills.

Every bill which shall have passed the House of Representatives and the Senate, shall, before it becomes a law, be presented to the President of the United States; if he approves he shall sign it, but if not he shall return it, with his objections to that House in which it shall have originated, who shall enter the objections at large on their journal, and proceed to reconsider it. If after such reconsideration two thirds of that House shall agree to pass the bill, it shall be sent, together with the objections, to the other House, by which it shall likewise be reconsidered, and if approved by two thirds of that House, it shall become a law. But in all such cases the votes of both Houses shall be determined by yeas and nays, and the names of the persons voting for and against the bill shall be entered on the journal of each House respectively. If any bill shall not be returned by the President within ten days (Sundays excepted) after it shall have been presented to him, the same shall be a law, in like manner as if he had signed it, unless the Congress by their adjournment prevent its return, in which case it shall not be a law.

Every order, resolution, or vote to which the concurrence of the Senate and House of Representatives may be necessary (except on a question of adjournment) shall be presented to the President of the United States; and before the same shall take effect, shall be approved by him, or being disapproved by him, shall be repassed by two thirds of the Senate and House of Representatives, according to the rules and limitations prescribed in the case of a bill.

Section 8. The Congress shall have power to lay and collect taxes, duties, imposts and excises, to pay the debts and provide for the common defense and general welfare of the United States; but all duties, imposts and excises shall be uniform throughout the United States;

To borrow money on the credit of the United States;

To regulate commerce with foreign nations, and among the several States, and with the Indian tribes;

To establish a uniform rule of naturalization, and uniform laws on the subject of bankruptcies throughout the United States;

To coin money, regulate the value thereof, and of foreign coin, and fix the standard of weights and measures;

To provide for the punishment of counterfeiting the securities and current coin of the United States;

To establish post offices and post roads;

To promote the progress of science and useful arts, by securing for limited times to authors and inventors the exclusive right to their respective writings and discoveries;

To constitute tribunals inferior to the Supreme Court;

To define and punish piracies and felonies committed on the high seas, and offenses against the law of nations;

To declare war, grant letters of marque and reprisal, and make rules concerning captures on land and water;

To raise and support armies, but no appropriation of money to that use shall be for a longer term than two years;

To provide and maintain a Navy;

To make rules for the government and regulation of the land and naval forces;

To provide for calling forth the militia to execute the laws of the Union, suppress insurrections and repel invasions;

To provide for organizing, arming, and disciplining the militia, and for governing such part of them as may be employed in the service of the United States, reserving to the states respectively, the appointment of the officers, and the authority of training the militia according to the discipline prescribed by Congress;

To exercise exclusive legislation in all cases whatsoever, over such District (not exceeding ten miles square) as may, by cession of particular states, and the acceptance of Congress, become the seat of the government of the United States, and to exercise like authority over all places purchased by the consent of the legislature of the state in which the same shall be, for the erection of forts, magazines, arsenals, dock-yards, and other needful buildings;—and

To make all laws which shall be necessary and proper for carrying into execution the foregoing powers, and all other powers vested by this Constitution in the government of the United States, or in any department or officer thereof.

Section 9. The migration or importation of such persons as any of the states now existing shall think proper to admit, shall not be prohibited by the Congress prior to the year one thousand eight hundred and eight, but a tax or duty may be imposed on such importation, not exceeding ten dollars for each person.

The privilege of the writ of habeas corpus shall not be suspended, unless when in cases of rebellion or invasion the public safety may require it.

No bill of attainder or ex post facto law shall be passed.

No capitation, or other direct, tax shall be laid, unless in proportion to the census or enumeration herein before directed to be taken.

No tax or duty shall be laid on articles exported from any state.

No preference shall be given by any regulation of commerce or revenue to the ports of one state over those of another: nor shall vessels bound to, or from, one state, be obliged to enter, clear, or pay duties in another.

No money shall be drawn from the Treasury, but in consequence of appropriations made by law; and a regular statement and account of the receipts and expenditures of all public money shall be published from time to time.

No title of nobility shall be granted by the United States: And no person holding any office of profit or trust under them, shall, without the consent of the Congress, accept of any present, emolument, office, or title, of any kind whatever, from any King, Prince, or foreign state.

Section 10. No state shall enter into any treaty, alliance, or confederation; grant letters of marque and reprisal; coin money; emit bills of credit; make any thing but gold and silver coin a tender in payment of debts; pass any bill of attainder, ex post facto law, or law impairing the obligation of contracts, or grant any title of nobility.

No state shall, without the consent of the Congress, lay any imposts or duties on imports or exports, except what may be absolutely necessary for executing its inspection laws: and the net produce of all duties and imposts, laid by any state on imports or exports, shall be for the use of the Treasury of the United States; and all such laws shall be subject to the revision and control of Congress.

No state shall, without the consent of Congress, lay any duty of tonnage, keep troops, or ships of war in time of peace, enter into any agreement or compact with another state, or with a foreign power, or engage in war, unless actually invaded, or in such imminent danger as will not admit of delay.

Article II

Section 1. The executive power shall be vested in a President of the United States of America. He shall hold his office during the term of four years, and, together with the Vice President, chosen for the same term, be elected, as follows:

Each state, shall appoint, in such manner as the legislature thereof may direct, a number of electors, equal to the whole number of Senators and Representatives to which the state may be entitled in the Congress; but no Senator or Representative, or person holding an office of trust or profit under the United States, shall be appointed an elector.

The electors shall meet in their respective states, and vote by ballot for two persons, of whom one at least shall not be an inhabitant of the same state with themselves. And they shall make a list of all the persons voted for, and of the number of votes for each; which list they shall sign and certify, and transmit sealed to the seat of the government of the United States, directed to the President of the Senate. The President of the Senate shall, in the presence of the Senate and House of Representatives, open all the certificates, and the votes shall then be counted. The person having the greatest number of votes shall be the President, if such number be a majority of the whole number of electors appointed; and if there be more than one who have such majority, and have an equal number of votes, then the House of Representatives shall immediately choose by ballot one of them for President; and if no person have a majority, then from the five highest on the list the said House shall in like manner choose the President. But in choosing the President, the votes shall be taken by states, the representation from each state having one vote; a quorum for this purpose shall consist of a member or members from two thirds of the states, and a majority of all the states shall be necessary to a choice.

In every case, after the choice of the President, the person having the greatest number of votes of the electors shall be the Vice President. But if there should remain two or more who have equal votes, the Senate shall choose from them by ballot the Vice President.

The Congress may determine the time of choosing the electors, and the day on which they shall give their votes; which day shall be the same throughout the United States.

No person except a natural born citizen, or a citizen of the United States, at the time of the adoption of this Constitution, shall be eligible to the office of President; neither shall any person be eligible to that office who shall not have attained to the age of thirty-five years, and been fourteen years a resident within the United States.

In case of the removal of the President from office, or of his death, resignation, or inability to discharge the powers and duties of the said office, the same shall devolve on the Vice President, and the Congress may by law provide for the case of removal, death, resignation, or inability, both of the President and Vice President, declaring what officer shall then act as President, and such officer shall act accordingly, until the disability be removed, or a President shall be elected. The President shall, at stated times, receive for his services, a compensation, which shall neither be increased nor diminished during the period for which he shall have been elected, and he shall not receive within that period any other emolument from the United States, or any of them.

Before he enters on the execution of his office, he shall take the following oath or affirmation:—"I do solemnly swear (or affirm) that I will faithfully execute the office of President of the United States, and will to the best of my ability, preserve, protect and defend the Constitution of the United States."

Section 2. The President shall be commander in chief of the Army and Navy of the United States, and of the militia of the several States, when called into the actual service of the United States; he may require the opinion, in writing, of the principal officer in each of the executive departments, upon any subject relating to the duties of their respective offices, and he shall have power to grant reprieves and pardons for offenses against the United States, except in cases of impeachment.

He shall have power, by and with the advice and consent of the Senate, to make treaties, provided two thirds of the Senators present concur; and he shall nominate, and by and with the advice and consent of the Senate, shall appoint ambassadors, other public ministers and consuls, judges of the Supreme Court, and all other officers of the United States, whose appointments are not herein otherwise provided for, and which shall be established by law: but the Congress may by law vest the appointment of such inferior officers, as they think proper, in the President alone, in the courts of law, or in the heads of departments.

The President shall have power to fill up all vacancies that may happen during the recess of the Senate, by granting commissions which shall expire at the end of their next session.

Section 3. He shall from time to time give to the Congress information of the state of the Union, and recommend to their consideration such measures as he shall judge necessary and expedient; he may, on extraordinary occasions, convene both Houses, or either of them, and in case of disagreement between them, with respect to the time of adjournment, he may adjourn them to such time as he shall think proper; he shall receive ambassadors and other public ministers; he shall take care that the laws be faithfully executed, and shall commission all the officers of the United States.

Section 4. The President, Vice President and all civil officers of the United States, shall be removed from office on impeachment for, and conviction of, treason, bribery, or other high crimes and misdemeanors.

Article III

Section 1. The judicial power of the United States, shall be vested in one Supreme Court, and in such inferior courts as the Congress may from time to time ordain and establish. The judges, both of the supreme and inferior courts, shall hold their offices during good behaviour, and shall, at stated times, receive for their services, a compensation which shall not be diminished during their continuance in office.

Section 2. The judicial power shall extend to all cases, in law and equity, arising under this Constitution, the laws of the United States, and treaties made, or which shall be made, under their authority;—to all cases affecting ambassadors, other public ministers and consuls;—to all cases of admiralty and maritime jurisdiction;—to controversies to which the United States shall be a party;—to controversies between two or more states;—between a state and citizens of another state;—between citizens of different states;—between citizens of the same state claiming lands under grants of different states, and between a state, or the citizens thereof, and foreign states, citizens or subjects.

In all cases affecting ambassadors, other public ministers and consuls, and those in which a state shall be a party, the Supreme Court shall have original jurisdiction. In all the other cases before mentioned, the Supreme Court shall have appellate jurisdiction, both as to law and fact, with such exceptions, and under such regulations as the Congress shall make.

The trial of all crimes, except in cases of impeachment, shall be by jury; and such trial shall be held in the state where the said crimes shall have been committed; but when not committed within any state, the trial shall be at such place or places as the Congress may by law have directed.

Section 3. Treason against the United States, shall consist only in levying war against them, or in adhering to their enemies, giving them aid and comfort. No person shall be convicted of treason unless on the testimony of two witnesses to the same overt act, or on confession in open court.

The Congress shall have power to declare the punishment of treason, but no attainder of treason shall work corruption of blood, or forfeiture except during the life of the person attained.

Article IV

Section 1. Full faith and credit shall be given in each state to the public acts, records, and judicial proceedings of every other state. And the Congress may by general laws prescribe the manner in which such acts, records and proceedings shall be proved, and the effect thereof.

Section 2. The citizens of each state shall be entitled to all privileges and immunities of citizens in the several states.

A person charged in any state with treason, felony, or other crime, who shall flee from justice, and be found in another state, shall on demand of the executive authority of the state from which he fled, be delivered up, to be removed to the state having jurisdiction of the crime.

No person held to service or labour in one state, under the laws thereof, escaping into another, shall, in consequence of any law or regulation therein, be discharged from such service or labour, but shall be delivered up on claim of the party to whom such service or labour may be due.

Section 3. New states may be admitted by the Congress into this Union; but no new state shall be formed or erected within the jurisdiction of any other state; nor any state be formed by the junction of two or more states, or parts of states, without the consent of the legislature of the states concerned as well as of the Congress.

The Congress shall have power to dispose of and make all needful rules and regulations respecting the territory or other property belonging to the United States; and nothing in this Constitution shall be so construed as to prejudice any claims of the United States, or of any particular state.

Section 4. The United States shall guarantee to every state in this Union a republican form of government, and shall protect each of them against invasion; and on application of the legislature, or of the executive (when the legislature cannot be convened) against domestic violence.

Article V

The Congress, whenever two thirds of both Houses shall deem it necessary, shall propose amendments to this Constitution, or on the application of the legislatures of two thirds of the several states, shall call a convention for proposing amendments, which, in either case, shall be valid to all intents and purposes, as part of this Constitution, when ratified by the legislatures of three fourths of the several States, or by conventions in three fourths thereof, as the one or the other mode of ratification may be proposed by the Congress; provided that no amendment which may be made prior to the year one thousand eight hundred and eight shall in any manner affect the first and fourth clauses in the Ninth Section of the First Article; and that no state, without its consent, shall be deprived of its equal suffrage in the Senate.

Article VI

All debts contracted and engagements entered into, before the adoption of this Constitution, shall be as valid against the United States under this Constitution, as under the Confederation.

This Constitution, and the laws of the United States which shall be made in pursuance thereof; and all treaties made, or which shall be made, under the authority of the United States, shall be the supreme law of the land; and the judges in every state shall be bound thereby, any thing in the Constitution or laws of any State to the contrary notwithstanding.

The Senators and Representatives before mentioned, and the members of the several state legislatures, and all executive and judicial officers, both of the United States and of the several states, shall be bound by oath or affirmation, to support this Constitution; but no religious test shall ever be required as a qualification to any office or public trust under the United States.

Article VII

The ratification of the conventions of nine states shall be sufficient for the establishment of this Constitution between the states so ratifying the same.

Done in convention by the unanimous consent of the states present the seventeenth day of September in the year of our Lord one thousand seven hundred and eighty seven and of the independence of the United States of America the twelfth. In witness whereof we have hereunto subscribed out names,

GO. WASHINGTON—*Presid't,*
and deputy from Virginia
Attest WILLIAM JACKSON *Secretary*

New Hampshire

| JOHN LANGDON | NICHOLAS GILMAN |

Massachusetts

| NATHANIEL GORHAM | RUFUS KING |

Connecticut

| WM. SAML. JOHNSON | ROGER SHERMAN |

New York

ALEXANDER HAMILTON

New Jersey

| WIL. LIVINGSTON | WM. PATERSON |
| DAVID BREARLEY | JONA. DAYTON |

Pennsylvania

B. FRANKLIN	THOS. FITZSIMONS
THOMAS MIFFLIN	JARED INGERSOLL
ROBT MORRIS	JAMES WILSON
GEO. CLYMER	GOUV MORRIS

Delaware

GEO. READ	RICHARD BASSETT
GUNNING BEDFORD JUN	JACO. BROOM
JOHN DICKINSON	

Maryland

JAMES MCHENRY	DANL CARROLL
DAN OF ST THOS.	
JENIFER	

Virginia

| JOHN BLAIR— | JAMES MADISON JR. |

North Carolina

| WM. BLOUNT | HU WILLIAMSON |
| RICHD. DOBBS SPAIGHT | |

South Carolina

J. RUTLEDGE	CHARLES PICKNEY
CHARLES COTESWORTH	PIERCE BUTLER
PICKNEY	

Georgia

| WILLIAM FEW | ABR BALDWIN |

Amendments

Article I

Congress shall make no law respecting an establishment of religion, or prohibiting the free exercise thereof; or abridging the freedom of speech, or of the press; or the right of the people peaceably to assemble, and to petition the government for a redress of grievances.

Article II

A well-regulated militia, being necessary to the security of a free state, the right of the people to keep and bear arms, shall not be infringed.

Article III

No soldier shall, in time of peace be quartered in any house, without the consent of the owner, nor in time of war, but in a manner to be prescribed by law.

Article IV

The right of the people to be secure in their persons, houses, papers, and effects, against unreasonable searches and seizures, shall not be violated, and no warrants shall issue, but upon probable cause, supported by oath or affirmation, and particularly describing the place to be searched, and the persons or things to be seized.

Article V

No person shall be held to answer for a capital, or otherwise infamous crime, unless on a presentment or indictment of a Grand Jury, except in cases arising in the land or naval forces, or in the militia, when in actual service in time of war or public danger; nor shall any person be subject for the same offense to be twice put in jeopardy of life or limb; nor shall be compelled in any criminal case to be a witness against himself, nor be deprived of life, liberty, or property, without due process of law; nor shall private property be taken for public use, without just compensation.

Article VI

In all criminal prosecutions, the accused shall enjoy the right to a speedy and public trial, by an impartial jury of the state and district wherein the crime shall have been committed, which district shall have been previously ascertained by law, and to be informed of the nature and cause of the accusation; to be confronted with the witnesses against him; to have compulsory process for obtaining witnesses in his favor, and to have the assistance of counsel for his defense.

Article VII

In suits at common law, where the value in controversy shall exceed twenty dollars, the right of trial by jury shall be preserved, and no fact tried by a jury, shall be otherwise reexamined in any court of the United States, than according to the rules of the common law.

Article VIII

Excessive bail shall not be required, nor excessive fines imposed, nor cruel and unusual punishments inflicted.

Article IX

The enumeration in the Constitution, of certain rights, shall not be construed to deny or disparage others retained by the people.

Article X

The powers not delegated to the United States by the Constitution, nor prohibited by it to the states, are reserved to the states respectively, or to the people.

Article XI

The judicial power of the United States shall not be construed to extend to any suit in law or equity, commenced or prosecuted against one of the United States by citizens of another state, or by citizens or subjects of any foreign state.

Article XII

The electors shall meet in their respective states, and vote by ballot for President and Vice President, one of whom, at least, shall not be an inhabitant of the same state with themselves; they shall name in their ballots the person voted for as President, and in distinct ballots the person voted for as Vice President, and they shall make distinct lists of all persons voted for as President, and of all persons voted for as Vice President, and of the number of votes for each, which lists they shall sign and certify, and transmit sealed to the seat of the government of the United States, directed to the President of the Senate;— The President of the Senate shall, in the presence of the Senate and House of Representatives, open all the certificates and the votes shall then be counted;—The person having the greatest number of votes for President, shall be the President, if such number be a majority of the whole number of electors appointed; and if no person have such majority, then from the persons having the highest numbers not exceeding three on the list of those voted for as President, the House of Representatives shall choose immediately, by ballot, the President. But in choosing the President, the votes shall be taken by states, the representation from each state having one vote; a quorum for this purpose shall consist of a member or members from two-thirds of the states, and a majority of all the states shall be necessary to a choice. And if the House of Representatives shall not choose a President whenever the right of choice shall devolve upon them, before the fourth day of March next following, then the Vice President shall act as President, as in the case of the death or other constitutional disability of the President.—The person having the greatest number of votes as Vice President, shall be the Vice President, if such number be a majority of the whole number of electors appointed, and if no person have a majority, then from the two highest numbers on the list, the Senate shall choose the Vice President; a quorum for the purpose shall consist of two-thirds of the whole number of Senators, and a majority of the whole number shall be necessary to a choice. But no person constitutionally ineligible to the office of President shall be eligible to that of Vice President of the United States.

Article XIII

Section 1. Neither slavery nor involuntary servitude, except as a punishment for crime whereof the party shall have been duly convicted, shall exist within the United States, or any place subject to their jurisdiction.

Section 2. Congress shall have power to enforce this article by appropriate legislation.

Article XIV

Section 1. All persons born or naturalized in the United States, and subject to the jurisdiction thereof, are citizens of the United States and of the state wherein they reside. No state shall make or enforce any law which shall abridge the privileges or immunities of citizens of the United States; nor shall any state deprive any person of life, liberty, or property, without due process of law; nor deny to any person within its jurisdiction the equal protection of the laws.

Section 2. Representatives shall be apportioned among the several states according to their respective numbers, counting the whole number of persons in each state, excluding Indians not taxed. But when the right to vote at any election for the choice of electors for President and Vice President of the United States, Representatives in Congress, the executive and judicial officers of a state, or the members of the legislature thereof, is denied to any of the male inhabitants of such state, being twenty-one years of age, and citizens of the United States, or in any way abridged, except for participation in rebellion, or other crime, the basis of representation therein shall be reduced in the proportion which the number of such male citizens shall bear to the whole number of male citizens twenty-one years of age in such state.

Section 3. No person shall be a Senator or Representative in Congress, or elector of President and Vice President, or hold any office, civil or military, under the United States, or under any state, who, having previously taken an oath, as a member of Congress, or as an officer of the United States, or as a member of any state legislature, or as an executive or judicial officer of any state, to support the Constitution of the United States, shall have engaged in insurrection or rebellion against the same, or given aid or comfort to the enemies thereof. But Congress may by a vote of two-thirds of each house, remove such disability.

Section 4. The validity of the public debt of the United States, authorized by law, including debts incurred for payment of pensions and bounties for services in suppressing insurrection or rebellion, shall not be questioned. But neither the United States nor any state shall assume or pay any debt or obligation incurred in aid of insurrection or rebellion against the United States, or any claim for the loss or emancipation of any slave; but all such debts, obligations and claims shall be held illegal and void.

Section 5. The Congress shall have power to enforce, by appropriate legislation, the provisions of this article.

Article XV

Section 1. The right of citizens of the United States to vote shall not be denied or abridged by the United States or by any state on account of race, color, or previous conditions of servitude—

Section 2. The Congress shall have power to enforce this article by appropriate legislation.

Article XVI

The Congress shall have power to lay and collect taxes on incomes, from whatever source derived, without apportionment among the several states, and without regard to any census or enumeration.

Article XVII

Section 1. The Senate of the United States shall be composed of two Senators from each state, elected by the people thereof, for six years; and each Senator shall have one vote. The electors in each state shall have the qualifications requisite for electors of the most numerous branch of the state legislatures.

Section 2. When vacancies happen in the representation of any state in the Senate, the executive authority of such state shall issue writs of election to fill such vacancies: *Provided,* That the legislature of any state may empower the executive thereof to make temporary appointments until the people fill the vacancies by election as the legislature may direct.

Section 3. This amendment shall not be so construed as to affect the election or term of any Senator chosen before it becomes valid as part of the Constitution.

Article XVIII

Section 1. After one year from the ratification of this article the manufacture, sale, or transportation of intoxicating liquors within, the importation thereof into, or the exportation thereof from the United States and all territory subject to the jurisdiction thereof for beverage purposes is hereby prohibited.

Section 2. The Congress and the several states shall have concurrent power to enforce this article by appropriate legislation.

Section 3. This article shall be inoperative unless it shall have been ratified as an amendment to the Constitution by the legislatures of the several states, as provided in the Constitution, within seven years from the date of the submission hereof to the states by the Congress.

Article XIX

Section 1. The right of citizens of the United States to vote shall not be denied or abridged by the United States or by any state on account of sex.

Section 2. Congress shall have power to enforce this article by appropriate legislation.

Article XX

Section 1. The terms of the President and Vice President shall end at noon on the 20th day of January, and the terms of Senators and Representatives at noon on the 3d day of January, of the years in which such terms would have ended if this article had not been ratified; and the terms of their successors shall then begin.

Section 2. The Congress shall assemble at least once in every year, and such meeting shall begin at noon on the 3d day of January, unless they shall by law appoint a different day.

Section 3. If, at the time fixed for the beginning of the term of the President, the President elect shall have died, the Vice President elect shall become President. If a President shall not have been chosen before the time fixed for the beginning of his term, or if the President elect shall have failed to qualify, then the Vice President elect shall act as President until a President shall have qualified; and the Congress may by law provide for the case wherein neither a President elect nor a Vice President elect shall have qualified, declaring who shall then act as President, or the manner in which one who is to act shall be selected, and such person shall act accordingly until a President or Vice President shall have qualified.

Section 4. The Congress may by law provide for the case of the death of any of the persons from whom the House of Representatives may choose a President whenever the right of choice shall have devolved upon them, and for the case of the death of any of the persons from whom the Senate may choose a Vice President whenever the right of choice shall have devolved upon them.

Section 5. Sections 1 and 2 shall take effect on the 15th day of October following the ratification of this article.

Section 6. This article shall be inoperative unless it shall have been ratified as an amendment to the Constitution by the legislatures of three- fourths of the several states within seven years from the date of its submission.

Article XXI

Section 1. The eighteenth article of amendment to the Constitution of the United States is hereby repealed.

Section 2. The transportation or importation into any state, territory, or possession of the United States for delivery or use therein of intoxicating liquors, in violation of the laws thereof, is hereby prohibited.

Section 3. This article shall be inoperative unless it shall have been ratified as an amendment to the Constitution by conventions in the several states, as provided in the Constitution, within seven years from the date of the submission hereof to the states by the Congress.

Article XXII

Section 1. No person shall be elected to the office of the President more than twice, and no person who has held the office of President, or acted as President, for more than two years of a term to which some other person was elected President shall be elected to the office of the President more than once. But this Article shall not apply to any person holding the office of President when this Article was proposed by the Congress, and shall not prevent any person who may be holding the office of President, or acting as President, during the term within which this Article becomes operative from holding the office of President or acting as President during the remainder of such term.

Section 2. This Article shall be inoperative unless it shall have been ratified as an amendment to the Constitution by the legislatures of three fourths of the several states within seven years from the date of its submission to the states by the Congress.

Article XXIII

Section 1. The District constituting the seat of government of the United States shall appoint in such manner as the Congress may direct:

A number of electors of President and Vice President equal to the whole number of Senators and Representatives in Congress to which the District would be entitled if it were a state, but in no event more than the least populous state; they shall be in addition to those appointed by the states, but they shall be considered, for the purposes of the election of President and Vice President, to be electors appointed by a state; and they shall meet in the District and perform such duties as provided by the twelfth article of amendment.

Section 2. The Congress shall have power to enforce this article by appropriate legislation.

Article XXIV

Section 1. The right of citizens of the United States to vote in any primary or other election for President or Vice President, for electors for President or Vice President, or for Senator or Representative in Congress, shall not be denied or abridged by the United States or any State by reason of failure to pay any poll tax or other tax.

Section 2. The Congress shall have power to enforce this article by appropriate legislation.

Article XXV

Section 1. In case of the removal of the President from office or of his death or resignation, the Vice President shall become President.

Section 2. Whenever there is a vacancy in the office of the Vice President, the President shall nominate a Vice President who shall take office upon confirmation by a majority vote of both Houses of Congress.

Section 3. Whenever the President transmits to the President pro tempore of the Senate and the Speaker of the House of Representatives his written declaration that he is unable to discharge the powers and duties of his office, and until he transmits to them a written declaration to the contrary, such powers and duties shall be discharged by the Vice President as Acting President.

Section 4. Whenever the Vice President and a majority of either the principal officers of the executive departments or of such other body as Congress may by law provide, transmit to the President pro tempore of the Senate and the Speaker of the House of Representatives their written declaration that the President is unable to discharge the powers and duties of his office, the Vice President shall immediately assume the power and duties of the office as Acting President.

Thereafter, when the President transmits to the President pro tempore of the Senate and the Speaker of the House of Representatives his written declaration that no inability exists, he shall resume the powers and duties of his office unless the Vice President and a majority of either the principal officers of the executive department or of such other body as Congress may by law provide, transmit within four days to the President pro tempore of the Senate and the Speaker of the House of Representatives their written declaration that the President is unable to discharge the powers and duties of his office. Thereupon Congress shall decide the issue, assemblying within forty-eight hours for that purpose if not in session. If the Congress, within twenty-one days after receipt of the latter written declaration, or, if Congress is not in session, within twenty-one days after Congress is required to assemble, determines by two-thirds vote of both Houses that the President is unable to discharge the powers and duties of his office, the Vice President shall continue to discharge the same as Acting President; otherwise, the President shall resume the powers and duties of his office.

Article XXVI

Section 1. The right of citizens of the United States, who are eighteen years of age or older, to vote shall not be denied or abridged by the United States or by any State on account of age.

Section 2. The Congress shall have power to enforce this article by appropriate legislation.

Article XXVII

No law varying the compensation for the service of Senators and Representatives shall take effect until an election of Representatives shall have intervened.

The Constitution

A Look at American History

For the examination, the following is all you need to know. This basic information is probably already familiar to you. If you want to study more, or to learn about what was going on in the world, that is here too. Check the chart on the pages following this brief summary.

What is now the United States began with the "discovery of America" by Christopher Columbus on October 12, 1492. Spanish settlements in the new world followed. Columbus Day is a legal holiday today.

In the 17th and early 18th centuries, the Dutch, the Swedes, the Germans, and the French established settlements here. The largest permanent settlements were made by the British. The first English colony was at Jamestown (Virginia) in 1607; the largest came soon after in 1620. There, the group we call the Pilgrims—about 100 men and women who sailed from England on the Mayflower—landed on what is now Massachusetts. They came for religious freedom and, after arriving on the cold coast of Cape Cod, drew up an agreement. The Mayflower Compact that they all signed promised to make laws for the good of all the settlers.

Other settlements followed. Within 100 years, there were 13 colonies along the East Coast of the new land. Although some people came from other countries, these colonies were dependent on England as their "mother country" and they were often referred to as the 13 English colonies and were required to pay taxes to England. Colonists found it hard to pay these taxes as they became higher and higher. Some felt taxation without representation was wrong. They protested, and England sent troops to enforce the laws. That was the beginning of the War for Independence—the American Revolution. Some of the great leaders of that time were George Washington, Benjamin Franklin, Thomas Jefferson, and Patrick Henry.

The Fourth of July is the most important national holiday today. The Declaration of Independence was signed on July 4, 1776, and a new country was born. A copy of this document including signatures of delegates is in this book. Look at it now! George Washington, who had commanded the rebellious army, became the first President. The first government of the new country was established under Articles of Confederation, which proved ineffective and did not last. Changes were necessary. And so, delegates were selected to work on another plan of government. They worked hard at the Constitutional Convention in Philadelphia and completed the Constitution—the new plan of government—in 1787.

Some of the delegates included Benjamin Franklin, Alexander Hamilton, and James Madison, with George Washington presiding. The Constitution was then sent to the states for ratification (approval). In 1789 the Constitution was adopted. The United States of America was established. The Constitution is still the highest law of the land although it has been amended (changed) 27 times. You should be familiar with the words of the Preamble (beginning). "We the people of the United States, in order to form a more perfect Union, establish justice, insure domestic tranquility (peace), provide for the common defense, promote the general welfare, and secure the blessings of liberty to ourselves and our posterity (those who come after us), do ordain (enact by law) and establish this Constitution for the United States of America."

You should also know the Bill of Rights (the first 10 amendments). It is the highest law of the land that protects all of us Americans. See the text on page 82.

Political and Governmental

Military & Special Events

American Foreign Relations

I. PERIOD OF EXPLORATION AND COLONIZATION, TO

Political and Governmental		Military & Special Events		American Foreign Relations
1000	Most highly developed Pre-Columbian governments in America were those of Incas in Peru and Aztecs in Mexico.			
		1482	Portugal refused to support Columbus in proposed westward voyage.	
		1492	Columbus made first voyage to America.	
		1497	Cabot claimed North American coast for England.	
		1500	Cabral discovered Brazil.	
		1513	Balboa discovered the Pacific by crossing Isthmus of Panama.	
		1513	Ponce de Leon explored Florida.	
		1519-21	Cortes conquered Aztecs.	
		1512-22	Magellan circumnavigated the globe.	
		1524	Verazzano explored in Canada.	
		1531-35	Pizarro conquered Incas in Peru.	
		1533-41	Cartier explored along St. Lawrence River.	
		1539	De Soto began exploration in North America.	
		1540-42	Coronado explored present southwestern United States.	
		1565 ★	St. Augustine, Florida, founded.	
		1585-87 ★	Raleigh sent expeditions to colonize Roanoke Island.	
		1607 ★	Jamestown founded.	
		1608	Quebec founded.	
1609	Virginia received new charter.	1609	Santa Fe founded.	
1619 ★	First legislature in Virginia.			
1624 ★	Virginia became royal colony.	1624	New Amsterdam (N.Y.) founded.	
		1630	Massachusetts Bay Colony founded.	
		1634	Maryland settled.	

Economic and Technological

Cultural and Intellectual

Parallel Events In World History

1763

Economic and Technological	Cultural and Intellectual	Parallel Events In World History
		1000 Leif Erícson discovered Vinland.
		1095-1291 The Crusades fought.
		1460 Prince Henry of Portugal died.
		1487 Diaz rounded Cape of Good Hope.
		1493 ★ Treaty of Tordesillas fixed Line of Demarcation.
		1498 Vasco Da Gama sailed to India.
		1517 ★ Luther's Theses published.
		1519-1556 Charles V reigned in Europe.
		1534 ★ Henry VIII established Anglican Church.
		1577 Drake began circumnavigation of globe.
		1588 ★ Spanish Armada defeated.
		1598 ★ Edict of Nantes.
1612 Rolfe introduced superior variety of tobacco to Virginia.		**1618-48** ★ Thirty Years War.
1619 First slaves brought to Virginia.		
	1620 Pilgrims introduced Congregational churches to America.	
		1628 ★ Charles I signed Petition of Rights.

Political and Governmental

Military & Special Events

American Foreign Relations

Political and Governmental	Military & Special Events	American Foreign Relations
	1636 ★ Roger Williams settled Providence.	
	1636 Hooker settled Connecticut.	
	1638 Delaware settled.	
1639 ★ Fundamental Orders of Connecticut.		
1643 ★ New England Confederation organized.		
	1664 ★ New Netherlands captured by Duke of York.	
	1670 Charleston founded.	
	1675 King Phillip's War.	
1676 ★ Governor Berkeley recalled to England.	1676 ★ Bacon's Rebellion.	
1679 New Hampshire made separate colony.	1681 Pennsylvania granted to William Penn.	
	1682 LaSalle claimed the Mississippi for France.	
1688 Dominion of New England.		
	1690-97 King William's War.	
	1691 Plymouth absorbed by Massachusetts.	
	1702-13 ★ Queen Anne's War.	
1729 North Carolina made separate colony.		
	1733 ★ Georgia settled.	

Economic and Technological

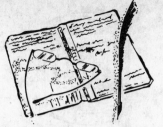

Cultural and Intellectual

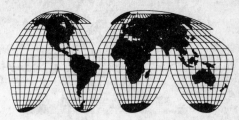

Parallel Events In World History

Economic and Technological	Cultural and Intellectual	Parallel Events In World History
	1636 Harvard University founded.	
	1639 Baptist church first organized in Rhode Island.	**1642-46** ★ Civil War in England.
		1643-1715 Louis XIV reign.
	1647 ★ Public elementary schools established by law in Massachusetts.	
1651 First navigation act passed.	**1649** ★ Maryland Religious Toleration Act passed.	
1660 Enumerated Commodities Act passed.		**1660** Charles II crowned King of England.
		1685 James I became King of England.
		1685 ★ Edict of Nantes revoked in France.
		1689 ★ William of Orange crowned King of England, in Glorious Revolution; Bill of Rights.
		1689-97 War of League of Augsburg.
	1692 Witchcraft trials at Salem.	
1696 Navigation Act passed.	**1693** William and Mary College founded.	
1697 Triangular trade began.		**1697** ★ Treaty of Ryswick.
1699 Woolens Act passed.		
1700 Rice became Carolina export staple.	**1701** Yale founded.	
	1704 *Boston News Letter* published.	**1702-13** ★ War of Spanish Succession.
		1713 ★ Peace of Utrecht.
		1715-74 Louis XV reigned in France.
1732 Hat Act passed.	**1732** *Poor Richard's Almanac* began.	
1733 Molasses Act.		
	1735 ★ Zenger Trial.	
	1740 Great Awakening centered about this time.	**1740-48** War of Austrian Succession.

153

**Political and Governmental**	**Military & Special Events**	**American Foreign Relations**
	1744-48 King George's War.	
1751 Georgia became royal colony.		
1754 ★ Albany Congress.	1754-63 ★ French and Indian War.	
	1755 Braddock's defeat.	
	1759 ★ Fall of Quebec.	
	1760 ★ British take Montreal.	
1761 ★ Writs of Assistance protested by James Otis.		
1763 Proclamation Act established Indian reserve in the West.		

II. ERA OF THE AMERICAN REVOLUTION AND THE

1763 ★ Paxton Boys.	1763 ★ Pontiac's War.	
1764 ★ Sugar Act.		
1765 ★ Stamp Act.	1765 ★ Stamp Act Congress.	
1765 ★ Quartering Act and repeal of Stamp Act.		
1766 ★ Declaratory Act.		
1767 ★ Townshend Acts.		
	1768-71 Regulator movements.	
	1769 Spanish colonize California.	
1770 Townshend Acts repealed except tea tax.	1770 ★ Boston Massacre.	
1772 ★ Committees of Correspondence organized.	1772 ★ Gaspée burned.	
1773 Tea Act.	1773 ★ Boston Tea Party.	
	1774 Lord Dunmore's (Indian) War in Kentucky.	
1774 ★ Intolerable Acts and Quebec Act.		
1774 ★ First Continental Congress met.		
1775 ★ Second Continental Congress met.	1775 Battles of Lexington, Concord, and Bunker Hill.	
1776 Declaration of Independence.	1776 Washington lost Battle of Long Island.	
	1776-83 American Revolution.	
1777 ★ Articles of Confederation submitted to states.	1777 ★ Battle of Saratoga.	
	1777-78 Washington at Valley Forge.	

Economic and Technological

Cultural and Intellectual

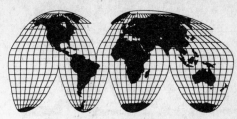

Parallel Events In World History

1747 Franklin began experiments with electricity.		**1748** ★ Treaty of Aix-la-Chapelle.
1750 Iron Act passed.		
		1756-63 ★ Seven Years War.
		1758 ★ William Pitt Prime Minister.
		1760-1820 Reign of George III.

CONFEDERATION, 1763-89

		1763 Treaty of Paris.
1764 Parliament forbade colonial paper money by Currency Act.		
		1770 Lord North made Prime Minister in England.
		1774-92 Louis XVI reigned in France.
1775 First American submarine built.		
	1776 ★ Thomas Paine wrote *Common Sense*.	**1776** ★ Adam Smith published *Wealth of Nations*.

Political and Governmental	Military & Special Events	American Foreign Relations

Political and Governmental	Military & Special Events	American Foreign Relations
	1778 British land at Savannah.	**1778** ★ Treaty of Alliance with France signed.
	1778-79 ★ Clark captured British posts in the Northwest Territory.	
1781 ★ Articles of Confederation ratified.	**1781** ★ Cornwallis captured at Yorktown.	
		1783 ★ Treaty of Paris recognized American independence.
1785 Land Ordinance enacted.	**1786** ★ Shays' Rebellion.	**1785** ★ Jay-Gardoqui Treaty negotiated but failed of ratification.
1787 ★ Northwest Ordinance enacted.		
1787 ★ Constitutional Convention met at Philadelphia.		
1788 Constitution ratified.		

III. EARLY NATIONAL PERIOD, 1789-1828

Political and Governmental	Military & Special Events	American Foreign Relations
1789 Washington inaugurated president.		
1789 ★ Judiciary Act.		
1790 National capital moved to Philadelphia.		
1791 ★ Whiskey Tax.		
1791 ★ Bill of Rights.		
1791 Vermont, first state admitted.		
1792 Kentucky admitted.		
		1793 Washington proclaimed neutrality; Citizen Genet's recall demanded.
	1794 ★ Whiskey Rebellion.	**1794** ★ Jay Treaty.
	1795 Treaty of Greenville ended Indian wars in Northwest.	**1795** ★ Pinckney Treaty.
1797-1801 John Adams president.		**1797** ★ XYZ Affair.
1798 ★ Alien and Sedition Acts; Kentucky and Virginia Resolutions.	**1798-99** ★ Undeclared naval war with France.	
1800 Capitol removed to Washington.		
1800 Jefferson elected president.		
		1800 Alliance with France abrogated.
		1800 Louisiana transferred to France.
	1801-05 ★ War with Tripoli.	
1803 ★ *Marbury v. Madison.*		**1803** ★ Louisiana Purchase Treaty.
1804 ★ 12th Amendment ratified.	**1804** Hamilton-Burr duel.	
	1804-06 ★ Lewis and Clark Expedition.	
		1805 ★ Essex decision.
	1806 Burr expedition.	**1806** ★ Berlin decrees.

Economic and Technological

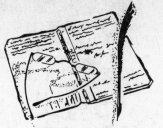

Cultural and Intellectual

Parallel Events In World History

Economic and Technological	Cultural and Intellectual	Parallel Events In World History
1784 Depression in America.	**1784** Methodist Church in America organized.	
1789 ★ First tariff act.		**1789** French Revolution began.
1790 Slater built first textile mill.		
1791 ★ Bank of the United States chartered.		
1793 Cotton gin invented.		**1793** Louis XVI beheaded.
		1793-94 French "Reign of Terror."
1794 Lancaster Turnpike completed.		
	1797 Great Revivals began.	
		1799 Napoleon became first consul.
		1803 Napoleon renewed war in Europe.
		1804 Napoleon made Emperor.

Political and Governmental

Military & Special Events

American Foreign Relations

Political and Governmental		Military & Special Events		American Foreign Relations	
		1807	★ *Chesapeake-Leopard* Affair.	1807	★ Embargo Act.
				1809	★ Non-intercourse Act.
1810	★ *Fletcher v. Peck.*			1810	★ Macon's Bill.
		1812	War begun against Great Britain.		
1814	★ Hartford Convention.	1814	British burned national capital.	1814	★ Treaty of Ghent ended War of 1812.
		1815	★ Jackson's victory at New Orleans.		
		1818	★ Rush-Bagot Agreement.		
1819	★ *McCulloch v. Maryland;* Dartmouth College case.			1819	★ Adams-Onis (Florida) Treaty.
1820	★ Missouri Compromise.				
1821	Missouri admitted.	1821	Stephen F. Austin began colonization of Texas.		
		1821	Santa Fe trade begun.		
1824	★ Adams defeated Jackson.			1823	★ Monroe Doctrine announced.
1824	★ *Gibbons v. Ogden.*				
1826	Antimasons organized.			1826	Panama Congress.
1828	★ Tariff of Abominations.			1827	Joint occupation of Oregon renewed.

Economic and Technological

Cultural and Intellectual

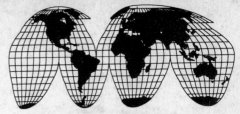

Parallel Events In World History

Economic and Technological	Cultural and Intellectual	Parallel Events In World History
1807 Embargo stimulated rise of American manufacturing.		
1807 *Clermont* steamed up the Hudson.		
1808 Foreign slave trade became illegal.		
		1810-22 ★ Wars for Latin American independence.
1811 National Road begun.		
	1815 U.S. population 9 million.	**1815** Battle of Waterloo and Congress of Vienna.
	1815-60 New England literary renaissance.	
1816 ★ Second Bank of the U.S. chartered; protective tariff passed.		
1817 ★ Bonus Bill vetoed.	**1817** American Colonization society organized.	
1817 Erie Canal begun.		
1819 Panic.		
1819 Cast iron plow.		
1820 Land Law revised.		
1820 New England ships became more active in California coastal trade.		
		1822 Latin American independence completed.
1825 ★ Erie Canal completed.	**1825** ★ Robert Owen founded New Harmony colony.	
1827 Baltimore & Ohio Railroad chartered.		
1830 *Tom Thumb* locomotive made trial run on B & O Railroad.		

Political and Governmental

Military & Special Events

American Foreign Relations

IV. AGE OF JACKSONIAN DEMOCRACY, 1828-50

Political and Governmental	Military & Special Events	American Foreign Relations
1830 ★ Webster-Hayne debates.		
1831 ★ Jackson reorganized Cabinet as result of Eaton Affair.		
1832 ★ Protective tariff maintained; Nullification Ordinance; Nullification Proclamation.	1832 Year of several fur expeditions to the Far West.	
1832 Jackson vetoed Bank Bill; Jackson reelected.	1832 ★ Black Hawk's War.	
1833 ★ Force Bill and Compromise Tariff.	1834 Rev. Lee started mission in Oregon.	
1836 ★ Specie circular issued.		1836 ★ Republic of Texas won independence.
1836 ★ Gag rule adopted.		
1837 Independent treasury defeated.	1837 ★ *Caroline* Affair.	1837 Texan independence recognized.
	1837-42 Seminole War.	
	1838 ★ Aroostook War.	
1840 ★ Harrison elected, first Whig president.		
1841 ★ Harrison died; Tyler became president.	1841 First pioneer settlers travelled overland to California.	
		1842 ★ Webster-Ashburton Treaty.
	1843 Large migration to Oregon.	1842 Commod. Jones seized Monterey, California.
1844 ★ Polk defeated Clay for president.		1845 Texas annexed.
		1845 Slidell mission sent to Mexico.
1846 ★ Wilmot Proviso first introduced.	1846-48 Mexican War.	
		1846 ★ Oregon Treaty.
	1847 Mormons began colonization of Utah.	
	1847 Scott marched to Mexico City.	
1848 Taylor elected president.	1848 Gold discovered at Sutter's mill.	1848 ★ Treaty of Guadalupe-Hidalgo.
1849 Department of Interior established.	1849 California Gold Rush.	

Economic and
Technological

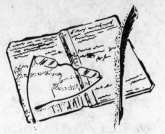

Cultural and
Intellectual

Parallel Events In
World History

Economic and Technological	Cultural and Intellectual	Parallel Events In World History
	1830 Mormon church organized.	**1830** July Revolutions; Louis Phillippe became King of France.
	1831 ★ Garrison began publication of *The Liberator*.	
	1831 ★ Nat Turner Rebellion.	**1832** First English Reform Bill.
	1833 Oberlin College founded.	
1835 Colt revolver patented.		
1835-36 Speculative boom and inflation.		
1837 Business panic followed by long depression.		**1837** Rebellion in Canada.
1837 Deere's steel plow.		
1841 ★ Preemption Act.		
1842 Courts recognized right of collective bargaining.		
1844 Morse constructed first telegraph line.	**1845** Poe published *The Raven*.	
1846 ★ Walker Tariff.		**1846** ★ Repeal of English Corn Laws.
1846 Howe invented sewing machine.		
1846 Ether used in surgery.		
		1848 Revolutions in Europe; *Communist Manifesto*.

Political and Governmental

Military & Special Events

American Foreign Relations

V. SECTIONAL STRIFE AND CIVIL WAR, 1850-65

Political and Governmental	Military & Special Events	American Foreign Relations
1850 Taylor died in office and was succeeded by Fillmore.		1850 ★ Clayton-Bulwer Treaty.
1850 ★ Compromise of 1850; California admitted.		
1852 Pierce inaugurated as president.		
		1853 ★ Gadsden Purchase Treaty.
1854 ★ Kansas-Nebraska Act; Republican Party organized.		1854 ★ Admiral Perry negotiated treaty with Japan.
		1854 ★ Ostend Manifesto.
	1856 Proslavery forces burned Lawrence, Kansas.	
1857 Buchanan inaugurated as president.	1857 Senator Sumner assaulted by Preston Brooks.	
1857 ★ Dred Scott.		
1857 ★ Lecompton constitution refused by Kansas.		
1858 ★ Lincoln-Douglas debates.		
	1859 ★ John Brown's Raid.	
1860 Lincoln elected president.	1860-61 Southern states seceded.	
1861 Lincoln inaugurated.	1861 Ft. Sumter surrendered; Civil War began; Battle of Bull Run.	1861 ★ Mason and Slidell taken from the *Trent*.
1861 Proposals of Peace Convention ignored.		1861 ★ Napoleon III intervened in Mexico.
1862 ★ Emancipation Proclamation issued.	1862 Battle of Antietam.	
1862 Homestead Act.		
	1863 Vicksburg taken by Grant; Lee defeated at Gettysburg.	
1864 ★ Lincoln vetoed Wade-Davis Bill.	1864 Wilderness Campaign; Sherman's march through Georgia.	

VI. RECONSTRUCTION PERIOD, 1865-77

Political and Governmental	Military & Special Events	American Foreign Relations
1865 Lincoln assassinated; Johnson became president.	1865 Lee surrendered at Appomattox.	
1865 ★ 13th Amendment ratified.	1865-85 Last Indian wars fought.	
1866 Civil Rights Bill passed.	1866 Race riots in the South.	1866 ★ Maximilian executed in Mexico.
1867 ★ Congressional Reconstruction Acts passed.		1867 ★ Alaska Purchase.

 Economic and Technological	 Cultural and Intellectual	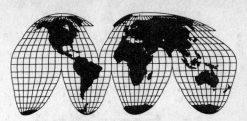 Parallel Events In World History
1850 First federal land grant to subsidize railroad building.	**1850** U.S. population reached 23 million.	
1851 Singer developed first practical sewing machine.	**1852** ★ *Uncle Tom's Cabin* published.	
		1854-56 Crimean War.
	1855 Amana colony settled in Iowa.	
1857 Business panic.	**1857** Helper's *Impending Crisis* published.	
1857 First overland stage line operated to California.		
1859 Oil industry began with "Drake's Folly."		**1859** Darwin published *Origin of the Species.*
1859 Pike's Peak and Comstock mining booms.		
1860-61 Pony Express.		
1861 Transcontinental (Pacific) Telegraph.		**1861** Russia emancipated serfs.
1861 ★ Morrill Tariff.		
1862 Union Pacific and Central Pacific railroads chartered.	**1862** ★ Morrill Land Grant College Act.	
1863 ★ National Banking Act passed.		
1864 First Pullman car built.		
1866 National Labor Union organized.		
1866 Atlantic cable operated successfully.		
1867 Farmers' Grange organized.		**1867** ★ Second Reform Bill adopted in Britain.

Political and Governmental

Military & Special Events

American Foreign Relations

Political and Governmental	Military & Special Events	American Foreign Relations
1868 ★ 14th Amendment ratified.		1868 ★ Burlingame Treaty with China.
1868 Johnson impeachment.		
1869 Grant inaugurated.	1869 "Black Friday" gold conspiracy.	
1870 ★ 15th Amendment ratified.		
1870-71 Enforcement acts passed against KKK.	1870 Legal Tender cases.	
	1871 Tweed Ring prosecuted.	1871 U.S. arrested Fenian leaders.
		1871 ★ Treaty of Washington.
1872 ★ Amnesty Act.	1872 ★ Crédit Mobilier scandal exposed.	
1872 Greeley defeated by Grant.		
1873 ★ "Salary Grab" Act.	1873 ★ Spain captured the *Virginius* off Cuba.	
1873 Grant began second term.		
1875 Greenback Party organized.		1875 Hawaiian Reciprocity Treaty.
1876 Hayes inaugurated as president. Southern Reconstruction ended.		

VII. THE CONSERVATIVE ERA, 1877-1901

Political and Governmental	Military & Special Events	American Foreign Relations
1879 ★ Denis Kearney active in California.		
1881 Garfield became president; assassinated; Arthur succeeded to presidency.		
1883 ★ Pendleton Act created Civil Service Commission.		

Economic and Technological

Cultural and Intellectual

Parallel Events In World History

Economic and Technological	Cultural and Intellectual	Parallel Events In World History
1867 Abilene, Kansas, first "cow-town" built.		
1868 ★ "Ohio Idea" proposed by Democrats in the election.		
1869 First transcontinental railroad completed.	**1869** Resurgence of temperance movement.	
1869 ★ Knights of Labor organized.		
		1871 Prussian victory over France in Treaty of Frankfurt; Germany united.
1872 Westinghouse airbrake put in use.		
1873 Business panic.	**1873** Kindergarten introduced.	
1873 ★ Silver demonetized in "Crime of '73."		
1873 Carnegie concentrated energies in steel business.		
1874 Large-scale manufacture of barbed wire began.	**1874** WCTU organized.	
1875 ★ Resumption Act passed.		
1876 Bell invented the telephone.		
1877 National railroad strike.		
1878 Twine binder invented.		
1878 ★ Bland-Allison Act.		
1879 ★ Gold standard resumed.	**1879** ★ Henry George published *Progress and Poverty*.	
1879 Standard Oil trust organized.	**1879** Christian Science founded.	
1881 ★ American Federation of Labor began.		
	1882 ★ Oriental immigration stopped.	
1883 Three more transcontinental railroads completed.		
1883 Downturn in cattle boom began.		**1883** Germany, Italy, and Austria form Triple Alliance.

Political and Governmental	Military & Special Events	American Foreign Relations
1885 Cleveland inaugurated.		
1886 ★ Wabash Decision.	1886 ★ Haymarket Riot.	
1887 ★ Interstate Commerce Commission created.		
1889 Harrison inaugurated as president.	1889-90 ★ Omnibus states admitted in the West.	1889 ★ First Pan-American Conference.
1889 Department of Agriculture created.	1890 American frontier substantially closed.	1889 ★ Fur Seal Controversy began.
1891 ★ Populist Party organized.		1891 ★ *Baltimore* crisis with Chile.
1893 Cleveland began second term.		1893 ★ Hawaiian monarchy overthrown.
1895 ★ Income tax declared unconstitutional.		1895 ★ Venezuelan boundary crisis.
1896 Hardest fought election in American politics.		
1897 McKinley inaugurated.		
	1898 Spanish-American War.	1898 ★ Treaty of Paris signed with Spain; Hawaii annexed.
	1899-1902 ★ Phillippine Insurrection.	1899 ★ Open Door Policy announced; First Hague Conference.
1900 McKinley reelected.	1900 ★ Boxer Uprising.	
1900 ★ Foraker Act established government in Puerto Rico.		

VIII. THE PROGRESSIVE ERA, 1901-1914

Political and Governmental	Military & Special Events	American Foreign Relations
1901 ★ McKinley assassinated; Roosevelt became president.		1901 ★ Platt Amendment imposed on Cuba; Hay-Pauncefote Treaty negotiated.
1902 ★ Newlands Reclamation Act.	1902 Insurrection in Phillippines suppressed.	1902 ★ Venezuelan debt controversy and Drago Doctrine.
1903 Department of Commerce and Labor created.		1903 ★ Hay-Herran Treaty with Columbia not ratified; Hay-Bunau-Varilla Treaty with Panama.
		1903 Alaskan Boundary dispute settled.

Economic and Technological

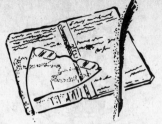

Cultural and Intellectual

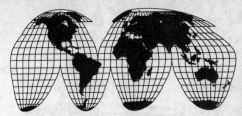

Parallel Events In World History

Economic and Technological	Cultural and Intellectual	Parallel Events In World History
1886 ★ Decline of Knights of Labor.		
1887 Hatch Act began establishment of agricultural experiment stations.	1887 Dawes Act.	
1890 ★ Sherman Silver Purchase Act, McKinley Tariff, and Sherman Antitrust Acts passed.		
1892 ★ Homestead strike.		1892 Dual Alliance of France and Russia formed.
1893 Business panic, followed by severe depression; Homestead strike.		
1894 Pullman strike; Coxey's Army; Wilson Tariff Act.		1894-95 Sino-Japanese War.
		1895 Cuban war for independence began.
		1895 Jameson Raid in South Africa.
1896 Klondike gold rush began.	1896 ★ *Plessy v. Ferguson* permitted segregated schools.	
1897 ★ Dingley Tariff.	1896 Marconi invented wireless telegraphy.	
		1899-1902 Boer War.
1900 ★ Gold Standard Act.	1900 U.S. population 75 million.	
1902 ★ Anthracite coal strike.		1902 ★ British-Japanese alliance.
1903 Wright brothers first successful flight.		
1903 ★ Elkins Act.		
1904 ★ Northern Securities case decided.		1904-05 Russo-Japanese War.

Political and Governmental	Military & Special Events	American Foreign Relations

1905 Roosevelt began second term.		1905 ★ Roosevelt helped negotiate Treaty of Portsmouth.
1906 Pure Food and Drug Act.		1906-07 ★ Algeciras Conference.
		1907 ★ Second Hague Conference.
1908 National Conservation Commission.		1908 ★ Root-Takahira Agreement.
1909 Taft inaugurated as President.		1909-13 "Dollar Diplomacy" of Taft administration.
1910 ★ Revolt against "Cannonism."		
1912 ★ "Bull Moose" Party in presidential election.	1912 Arizona and New Mexico admitted.	1912 ★ Panama Canal Tolls Act.
1913 Wilson inaugurated as president.		1913 ★ "Watchful Waiting" policy adopted against Huerta.
1913 ★ 16th and 17th Amendments added.		
1913 Department of Labor made separate.		

IX. THE WILSON ADMINISTRATION AND WORLD WAR I

1914 ★ Clayton Antitrust Act passed and Federal Trade Commission created.	1914 ★ American marines captured Vera Cruz.	
1916 Wilson reelected by narrow vote.	1916 ★ Marines sent to Santo Domingo.	
	1916 ★ Villa led border raid against Columbus, New Mexico.	1917 U.S. declared war on Germany.
		1917 ★ Lansing-Ishii Agreement.
		1917 Virgin Islands purchased from Denmark.
	1918 American Expeditionary Force active in battles on the Western Front.	1918 ★ Wilson announced Fourteen Points.
1919-20 ★ Congressional debates over Treaty of Versailles. Treaty rejected.		1919 ★ Wilson at Versailles Peace Conference.
1920 Presidential election, a "solemn referendum" and Republican landslide.		
1920 ★ Merchant Marine Act passed.		

Economic and Technological

Cultural and Intellectual

Parallel Events In World History

		1905	Revolution in Russia.
1906	Construction of Panama Canal began.		
1906 ★	Hepburn Act.		
1907	Brief money panic.		
1907	First radio broadcast.		
1908	Model "T" Ford developed.		
1909 ★	Payne-Aldrich Tariff.		
1910 ★	Mann-Elkins Act.	1910	Madero led revolution in Mexico.
1913 ★	Underwood Tariff and Federal Reserve Acts passed.	1913 ★	Huerta led counterrevolution in Mexico.

1913-21

1914	Panama Canal completed.			1914	Assassination of Archduke Ferdinand caused outbreak of World War I.
		1915 ★	"Grandfather" clauses declared unconstitutional.	1915 ★	British ship *Lusitania* sunk.
1916 ★	Federal Farm Loan Act and Adamson Railway Labor Acts passed.			1916 ★	French ship *Sussex* sunk.
				1917 ★	Mexico adopted new constitution.
		1918-19	Influenza epidemic caused 500,000 deaths in U.S.		
		1919 ★	18th Amendment ratified and Volstead Act passed.		
		1919-20	"Big Red Scare."		
1920 ★	Esch-Cummins Act returned railroads to private ownership.	1920 ★	19th Amendment gave vote to women.		

Political and Governmental

Military & Special Events

American Foreign Relations

X. THE CONSERVATIVE REPUBLICAN ERA, 1921-33

Political and Governmental	Military & Special Events	American Foreign Relations
1921 Harding inaugurated.		**1921** Separate American peace made with Germany, Austria, and Hungary.
1921 ★ Sacco-Vanzetti case began.		
		1921-22 ★ Washington Conference.
1923 Harding died; Coolidge succeeded to presidency.		
1923 Farm "bloc" became important factor in Congress.		
1924 Adjusted compensation ("bonus") voted for veterans.		**1924** ★ Dawes Plan adopted.
1924 ★ Teapot Dome scandal.		
1924 La Follette won 5 million votes in presidential election.		
1925 Coolidge began second term.		
1927 ★ Coolidge vetoed McNary-Haugen Bill.		**1927** ★ Morrow initiates friendly policy toward Mexico.
1928 Coolidge again vetoed McNary-Haugen farm relief.		**1928** ★ Kellogg-Briand Pact; failure of Geneva Disarmament Conference.
1929 Hoover inaugurated as president.		**1929** ★ Young Plan negotiated.
		1931 Hoover declared moratorium on international debts.
	1932 "Bonus army" driven out of Washington.	**1932** ★ Stimson Doctrine.

Economic and Technological

Cultural and Intellectual

Parallel Events In World History

Economic and Technological	Cultural and Intellectual	Parallel Events In World History
	1920 s — Decade of revolt against Victorianism in manners and morals.	
1921 — Primary postwar depression.	1921 ★ Emergency Immigration Act passed.	
1922 ★ Fordney-McCumber Tariff Act.		1922 — Mussolini rose to power.
	1924 ★ Basic immigration law passed.	
	1924 — Ku Klux Klan reached climax.	
1925 — Rust Brothers invent cotton picking machine.	1925 ★ Scopes trial.	
1926 — Radio came into popular use.	1926 — Sinclair Lewis published *Elmer Gantry.*	
1927 — Lindbergh solo flight to Paris.		
1928 — "Talking pictures" introduced.		
1929 ★ Stock market crash precipitated Great Depression.		
1929 — Agricultural Marketing Act created Federal Farm Board.		
	1930 s — Decade of the Great Depression and its blighting economic and social effects.	
1931 ★ Hawley-Smoot Tariff.		1931 ★ Japan invaded Manchuria.
1932 — Home Loan Bank Act.		

**Political and
Governmental**

**Military & Special
Events**

**American Foreign
Relations**

XI. THE NEW DEAL, 1933-39

Political and Governmental	Military & Special Events	American Foreign Relations
1933 FDR inaugurated in depth of Great Depression.		**1933** ★ Roosevelt launched "Good Neighbor" Policy.
1933 ★ 20th ("Lame Duck") Amendment ratified; 21st (prohibition repeal) Amendment ratified.		
1933 ★ Numerous New Deal relief, recovery, and reform measures passed: CCC, FERA, CWA, FCA, AAA, NRA, USES, TVA, HOLC, FDIC, and SEC (1934).		
		1934 Platt Amendment abrogated.
		1934 ★ Nye Committee investigated munitions industry; Johnson Act against debt defaulters.
1935 ★ "Second New Deal" begun: WPA created, Wagner Act, Wheeler-Rayburn Social Security established.	**1935** Last marines withdrawn from Haiti and Nicaragua.	**1935-37** Neutrality Act passed.
1936 ★ Soil Conservation Act; Merchant Marine Act.		
1937 ★ Supreme Court and F. D. Roosevelt.		
1937 Roosevelt began second term.		**1937** ★ Roosevelt delivered "Quarantine speech" against agressor nations.

XII. WORLD WAR II AND THE COLD WAR PERIOD

Political and Governmental	Military & Special Events	American Foreign Relations
		1939 Mutual security policies adopted at Panama City and Havana.
		1939 U.S. cancelled treaty of 1911 with Japan.
		1939 ★ Revision of Neutrality Acts permitted aid to Allies.
	1940 ★ Selective Service Act passed.	
1941 Roosevelt began third term.	**1941-42** Battle of the Atlantic against German submarines at its worst.	**1941** ★ Atlantic Charter announced by Roosevelt and Churchill; Lend-Lease Act passed.
	1941 ★ Attack on Pearl Harbor brought U.S. into World War II.	

Economic and Technological

Cultural and Intellectual

Parallel Events In World History

Economic and Technological	Cultural and Intellectual	Parallel Events In World History
1933 ★ National banking crisis.		1933 Hitler came to power in Germany.
1934 Reciprocal Trade Agreements Act.		
1934 ★ Tydings-McDuffie Act provided for Phillippine independence.		
1935 ★ Gold Clause Act nullified gold clauses in contracts.		1935 ★ Italy invaded Ethiopia.
1935 Drought and "dust bowl."		
1936-39 Sulfa drugs.	1936 *Gone With the Wind* published.	1936 Germany reoccupied Rhineland.
		1936 Rome-Berlin Alliance.
		1936 ★ Spanish Civil War began.
1937-38 Depression renewed; severe strikes occurred as labor sought union recognition.		1937 Japan opened war against China.
1938 ★ Fair Labor Standards Act.		1938 Germany annexed Austria, later Czechoslovakia.
		1939 German-Soviet nonaggression pact.
1939-52 Discovery and use of antibiotics.	1939 Steinbeck published *The Grapes of Wrath*.	1939 World War II began with Nazi invasion of Poland.
		1940 Nazis overran western Europe.
		1941 Hitler began invasion of Russia.
		1941 Japan won wide ranging victories over the Pacific and Far East.

Political and Governmental

Military & Special Events

American Foreign Relations

Political and Governmental	Military & Special Events	American Foreign Relations
	1942 ★ U.S. began counterattacks against Japan and Germany by invasions of Guadalcanal and North Africa.	**1943** Casablanca Conference demanded "unconditional surrender"; Moscow Conference agreed to formation of UNO.
	1944 ★ June 6 "D-Day" invasion of Normandy; Dec.-Jan., Battle of the Bulge.	**1944** ★ Yalta Conference on disposal of defeated powers and other problems.
	1944-45 ★ Phillippines reoccupied.	
1945 Roosevelt began 4th term and died soon thereafter; Truman succeeded to presidency.	**1945** May, Germany defeated. August, Japan surrendered.	**1945** ★ April, UNO charter drawn up at San Francisco; Potsdam Conference.
1946 Atomic Energy Commission created; Republicans won mid-term election; demobilization.	**1946** Overhasty demobilization of armed forces; peacetime conscription adopted.	**1946** International war crimes trials begun.
1947 ★ Presidential Succession Act.	**1947** Department of Defense formed by merger of War and Navy departments.	**1947** Peace treaties signed with minor powers.
		1947 ★ Truman Doctrine applied in Greece and Turkey.
		1947 ★ Marshall Plan (ECA) adopted by Congress.
1948 Presidential victory of Truman.	**1948** ★ Berlin blockade begun; ended in 1949.	
1949 Truman began second term; Fair Deal.	**1949** European rearmament under NATO	**1949** ★ North Atlantic Pact; Point Four program.
1949 ★ Communists convicted under Smith Act.		
1950 ★ McCarran Act against communists.	**1950** ★ Korean War began.	**1950s** Decade of recurring diplomatic crises.
1951 ★ 22nd Amendment (anti-third term) ratified.	**1951** McArthur recalled by Truman.	**1951** Peace treaty with Japan.
1952 Eisenhower carries Republicans to victory.	**1952** ★ ANZUS Treaty.	
1953 Eisenhower inaugurated.	**1953** Korean War ended in truce.	
1953 Department of HEW created.		
1954 ★ St. Lawrence Seaway Act passed.	**1954** Indo-China War ended by Geneva conference.	**1954** ★ St. Lawrence Seaway Act
	1954 ★ SEATO formed.	
	1955 ★ Geneva Summit Conference.	

Economic and Technological

Cultural and Intellectual

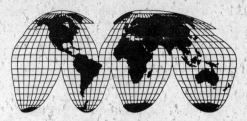

Parallel Events In World History

Economic and Technological	Cultural and Intellectual	Parallel Events In World History
		1943 Italy surrendered.
1945 ★ Atomic age began with successful bombing of Hiroshima and Nagasaki.		1945 Russia declared war on Japan.
1946 Year of prolonged strikes and inflation.		
1946 ★ Congress passed Full Employment Act.		
1947 Taft-Hartley Act.		1947 ★ Cominform organized.
1947 Television coming into wide use.		
		1948 Israel independence granted by Britain.
		1949 Indonesian independence recognized.
		1949 Republic of West Germany formed.
		1949 Russia exploded her first atomic bomb.
	1950 Social Security Act liberalized.	1950 Communists completed victory in China.
	1950 s Decade of the "Beat Generation," the "affluent society," and mass culture.	
1952 Truman confiscated steel industry during long strike.	1952 ★ McCarran-Walters Act revised immigration law.	
1953 Reciprocal Trade Agreements Act extended throughout Eisenhower administration.		
1953 Slight recession.		
1954 Capital goods boom began.	1954 ★ Supreme Court ruled separate schools unconstitutional; Social Security liberalized again.	1954 Sovereignty of West Germany recognized.
	1955 Labor fought for guaranteed annual wage; CIO-AFL merger.	1955 Peace treaty with Austria signed.

Political and Governmental	Military & Special Events	American Foreign Relations

Political and Governmental	Military & Special Events	American Foreign Relations
	1956 ★ Suez crisis	
1957 Eisenhower began second term.		1957 ★ Eisenhower Doctrine approved by Congress
	1958 Alaska admitted.	
	1958 Communist China shelled Quemoy and Natsu; American troops landed in Lebanon.	
	1959 Hawaii admitted.	

XIII. THE 1960s

Political and Governmental	Military & Special Events	American Foreign Relations
		1960 ★ U-2 incident.
1961 Kennedy inaugurated.	1961 ★ Bay of Pigs disaster in Cuba.	1961 ★ Crisis over Berlin.
1961 ★ 23rd Amendment ratified.		1961 ★ Alliance for Progress began in Latin-America; Peace Corps established.
1962 Kennedy clashed with steel industry.	1962 Crisis with Russia over missiles in Cuba.	1962 Almost all trade with Cuba banned.
1962 Midterm elections endorse Kennedy administration.		
1963 Kennedy tax reforms delayed in Congress.		1963 ★ Atomic test-ban treaty signed with Russia.
1963 Nov. 22, Kennedy assassinated; Johnson succeeded to Presidency.		
1964 24th Amendment (anti-poll tax) ratified; Supreme Court requires reapportionment of state legislatures; Johnson elected President over Goldwater.	1964 Escalation of war in Vietnam.	
1965 Johnson announces "The Great Society."	1965 Further escalation of war in Vietnam; U.S. Marines land in Dominican Republic.	1965 Immigration Act ended quotas based on national origin.
1966 ★ 25th Amendment ratified, dealing with presidential disability.	1967 Punta del Este Meeting of Western Hemisphere countries.	1965-66 Massive U.S. military aid to South Vietnam.
1967-68 ★ Long hot summers of urban riots.		
	1967 Johnson and Kosygin met at Glassboro Summit.	
1968 Assassination of Dr. Martin Luther King, Jr., civil rights leader, and Senator Robert F. Kennedy, candidate for president.		1968 Vietnam crisis pushed Johnson away from reelection attempt.
1968 Report of the National Advisory Commission on Civil Disorders.	1968 Vietnam preliminary peace talks began in Paris.	
1968 Johnson signed new Civil Rights Bill barring discrimination in housing.		

Economic and Technological

Cultural and Intellectual

Parallel Events In World History

		1956 Hungarian revolt crushed by Soviets.
	1957 ★ Civil Rights Act; Little Rock violence over school integration.	**1957** Russia launched Sputnik I.
1958 Economic recession.	**1958** ★ National Defense Education Act, federal funds for science, math, language, libraries.	
1959 ★ Landrum-Griffin Act to regulate labor unions.		**1959** Castro came to power in Cuba.
	1960 Stronger civil rights act passed.	
		1961 ★ Russians built Berlin wall.
1962 John Glenn rocketed into orbit; stock market panic and recovery.	**1962** Integration violence at Jackson, Mississippi.	
1963 Johnson won tax reductions from Congress.	**1963** National integration crisis worsened.	**1963** Rift between Russia and China widened.
	1964 ★ Civil Rights Act of 1964 passed.	**1964** Khrushchev deposed as Soviet leader.
1965 ★ Immigration Act		
1965 Johnson's "War on Poverty" curtailed by rising Vietnam costs.		
1966 ★ Medicare Act goes into operation.		**1966** France withdrew NATO troops.
		1966 Sukarno lost power in Indonesia.
	1967 New Metropolitan Opera House, New York, with giant murals by Marc Chagall.	**1967** ★ Israel defeated Arab states in Six-day war. Jerusalem reunited.
		1967 First heart transplant performed in South Africa by Dr. Barnard.
1968 In world monetary crisis U.S. agreed to two-price gold system.	**1968** Antiwar and left wing student rebellions widespread in U.S. and elsewhere.	**1968** Soviet Union invaded Czechoslovakia.
1968 Poor March on Washington led by Dr. Abernathy.	**1968** U.S. population passed 200 million.	**1968** A-Ban Treaty signed.
		1968 Biafran War in second year.
		1968 Pope Paul issued birth control ban.
		1969 Sporadic warfare continued between Israel and Egypt.

Political and Governmental

Military & Special Events

American Foreign Relations

Political and Governmental	Military & Special Events	American Foreign Relations
1968 Richard Nixon elected president. Spiro Agnew as vice president.	**1968** Apollo flight of eleven days.	**1968** U.S. Navy ship *Pueblo* seized by North Korea.
1969 Increased protests against war in Vietnam. U.S. troop withdrawals begun.	**1969** U.S. put first man on the moon.	**1968** Tet offensive against South Vietnam in the continuing war.
1969 Burger succeeded Warren as Chief Justice of the Supreme Court.	**1969** Vietnam War reduced in scale; widespread anti-war protests.	**1969** Nixon visited Romania in world trip.
	1969 U.S. and Russia signed N-Treaty.	

XIV. THE 1970s

Political and Governmental	Military & Special Events	American Foreign Relations
	1970 Vietnamization of Indochina conflict begun.	
1971 26th Amendment ratified lowering voting age to 18.	**1970** Cambodia invaded; demonstrating students killed at Kent State College.	
1972 Nixon reelected in overwhelming defeat of McGovern.		**1972** Common Market countries agreed to British entry.
1972 Watergate break-in at Democratic national headquarters.		**1972** ★ Summit conference at Peking. Nixon visited China ending 22 years of hostility.
1973 ★ Watergate scandal breaks.	**1973** Indian militants occupied village of Wounded Knee.	**1972** ★ Summit conference at Moscow. Nixon's visit to Moscow produced Strategic Arms Limitation Treaty (SALT).
1973 Agnew forced to resign over income tax evasion. Representative Gerald Ford of Michigan named new vice president.	**1973** U.S.-North Vietnam cease-fire agreement. U.S. troops withdrawn.	**1973** Yom Kippur War of Arab states against Israel ended by U.S. pressure for ceasefire.
1974 Top Nixon aides indicted for Watergate-related crimes; the president also named "unindicted co-conspirator."		
1974 Facing impeachment. Nixon resigned. Ford became president.		
1974 Ford pardoned Nixon one month after starting office.		
	1975 All of Vietnam fell under Communist control.	
1976 James E. Carter, former Democratic governor of Georgia, elected president.	**1976** U.S. Bicentennial widely celebrated.	
		1978 Panama Canal treaties signed ending U.S. operation and control.
		1978 Carter brought Egypt's Sadat and Israel's Begin to peace conference.

Economic and Technological

Cultural and Intellectual

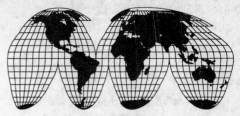

Parallel Events In World History

Economic and Technological	Cultural and Intellectual	Parallel Events In World History
	1968 Fair Housing Act barred racial discrimination in sales and rentals of most housing.	
1969 Nixon administration fought losing battle against inflation.	**1969** Woodstock, New York music and art fair attracted 300,000 enthusiasts.	**1969** President deGaulle of France resigned. Pompidou succeeded him.
		1969 Border hostilities between China and Soviet Union.
1970 Drastic declines in securities markets; interest rates peak to Civil War levels; increase in unemployment.		**1970** Heath became Prime Minister in Great Britain.
	1971 Publication of Pentagon Papers revealed Vietnam policy making procedures.	**1970** Allende, Marxist, elected President of Chile.
1971 Amtrak established to restore adequate rail service.	**1971** Two "new" galaxies discovered adjacent to earth's galaxy, the Milky Way.	**1971** People's Republic of China admitted into United Nations.
1971 Nixon announced "New Economic Policy" of wage and price controls.	**1971** Cigarette advertising banned from U.S. television.	
1972 Stimulative policies of government bring high level of economic activity in election year.		**1972** Bangladesh won independence from Pakistan.
1972-73 ★ Inflation and dollar devaluations.		
1973 ★ Energy crisis belatedly recognized.		**1973** Yom Kippur War, fourth between Arabs and Israel since 1948.
1973 Mid-East oil producers boycotted shipments to U.S., other nations friendly to Israel.		
1973-74 ★ Apollo spaceships docked with Skylab; much information collected.		
1974 OPEC (Organization of Petroleum Exporting Countries) quadrupled world crude oil prices. Expensive nuclear power plants begun.		
	1975 Brooklyn's Bobby Fischer gave up world chess championship.	
1976 Conrail combined ailing northeast railroads to revitalize freight service.	**1976** Episcopal Church approved ordination of women as priests and bishops.	
	1976 Increased concern that spray can gases damage earth atmosphere's ozone layer.	
1977-80 High inflation and large government expenditures hurt Carter's reelection chances.		**1977** President Sadat of Egypt visited Israel to discuss peace.

179

Political and Governmental

Military & Special Events

American Foreign Relations

		1979	Major nuclear power plant failure of Three Mile Island, Pennsylvania.

1979 — U.S. embassy and hostages seized at Teheran, Iran.

XV. THE 1980s

1980 Ronald Reagan unseated President Carter in landslide election victory.

1980 — Aborted attempt to rescue American hostages by helicopter.

1981 Sandra Day O'Connor named first female Supreme Court Justice.

1983 CIA mined Nicaraguan harbors.

1983 U.S. troops invaded eastern Caribbean island of Grenada.

1983 U.S. arms aid to anti-Sandinista contras to topple Nicaraguan government.

1983 Loss of 242 U.S. marines in Beirut, Lebanon, terrorist attack.

1984 Reagan and Bush easily re-elected over Walter Mondale.

1985 Congress passed Gramm-Rudman Act requiring reductions in government spending (Balanced Budget Act).

1985 Reagan paid controversial visit to German military cemetery at Bitburg.

1986 Explosion of shuttle *Challenger* shelved U.S. manned space program.

1986 U.S. warplanes bombed Tripoli, Libya to punish open support of terrorist activities.

**Economic and Technological**	**Cultural and Intellectual**	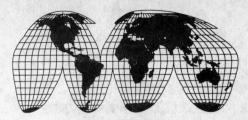**Parallel Events In World History**
		1979 Moslem fundamentalists overthrew monarchy in Iran.
		1979 Soviet troops invaded Afghanistan, chilling détente.
		1979 Nicaraguan *Sandinistas* ousted repressive military regime of Anastasio Somoza.
	1980 Alaska Lands Conservation Act doubled area of U.S. national parks.	1980-84 Civil War in El Salvador pitted President Duarte against leftist insurgents.
	1980s Social changes noted from 1970s on—Americans more aware of needs and problems of senior citizens and the handicapped; number of women employed in medicine and the sciences grew dramatically; and 40% of population increase was in three states of Texas, Florida, and California.	1980 Iran-Iraq war started; replaced Israel as main Arab problem.
	1980s School reform movement focused national attention on the importance and purposes of effective instruction.	
	1980s Epidemic spread of AIDS sparked medical research for treatment and cure.	
1981 Congress cuts social programs: Medicare, food stamps, college student loans, mass transit.		
1981 Reagan administration advocated supply-side economics and higher military spending.		
1981-84 Reaganomics led to doubling of the national debt.		
		1982 Israeli invasion of Lebanon forced out Arafat's PLO terrorists.
		1984 Drought and poverty caused widespread famine in Africa.
1985 Previously world's largest creditor, U.S. became a debtor.	1985 Televised Live Aid concerts involved millions worldwide in famine relief for Africans.	1985 Americans and Europeans kidnapped and held hostage in Lebanon.
		1986 Corazon Aquino defeated dictator Ferdinand Marcos for Philippine presidency.

 Political and Governmental	 Military & Special Events	 American Foreign Relations
	1986 Reagan proposed Star Wars (Strategic Defense Initiative) research and deployment plan.	
1987 Iran-Contra scandal exposed arms for hostages deal; illegal covert activities.	**1987** U.S. Navy began escorting Kuwaiti oil tankers through Persian Gulf.	**1987** U.S.-USSR treaty to ban, destroy many nuclear missiles in Europe.
1987 Reagan's Supreme Court nominations of Robert Bork and Douglas Ginsburg defeated.	**1987** Bicentennial of U.S. Constitution sparked renewed study of our basic law.	
1988 George Bush and Dan Quayle were elected to the presidency and vice presidency.	**1988** Terrorists killed nine tourists on a cruise in the Aegean Sea.	**1988** U.S.A. and Canada reached a free trade agreement.
1988 Congress overrode Reagan's veto of the Civil Rights Bill.	**1988** Lieutenant Colonel Higgins, an American army officer, kidnapped in Lebanon and later murdered.	
1989 George Bush inaugurated as the 41st president.	**1989** American troops invaded Panama to capture General Manuel Noriega, resulting in damage and harm to population.	**1989** President Bush and Mikhail Gorbachev, President of the U.S.S.R., met on a ship off the coast of Malta for a summit conference.
		1989 Berlin Wall torn down, allowing free travel in Germany.

XVI. THE 1990s

1990 Democrats gained control of the House of Representatives and the Senate.	**1990** General Noriega surrendered to American troops in Panama.	**1990** Western Alliance ended Cold War and began plans for joint action with U.S.S.R. and East Germany.
1990 Inquiry began into the role of five U.S. senators in the failure of savings and loan banks.	**1990** U.S. entered Persian Gulf War.	
1990 Bush appointed Judge David H. Souter to the Supreme Court upon the retirement of Justice William Brennan.		
1991 Clarence Thomas became 106th Justice of the Supreme Court.		**1991** International Conference on Global Warming, a threat to life on Earth, held in Geneva, Switzerland.
1991 Haitians who entered U.S.A. were detained at Guantanamo Bay for return to Haiti because they were said to be economic, not political refugees.		
1992 President Bush went to the Far East to try to obtain trade agreements that would benefit Americans.	**1992** Five-hundreth anniversary of Columbus's landing in America. **1992** Operation Restore Hope in Somalia.	**1992** United Nations requested Libya to extradite two suspects in 1988 bombing of Pan Am flight 103, which crashed in Scotland.
1992 CORE (the Congress of Racial Equality) accused of fraud in preparing amnesty applications for aliens under the 1986 Immigration Reform and Control Act. Suit entered by the Federal Immigration Bar Association.		**1992** Chilean arms shipment to Croatia declared in violation of U.N. ban on such shipments. Material intercepted in Budapest, Hungary.

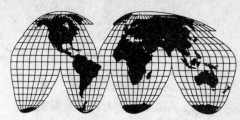

Economic and Technological

Cultural and Intellectual

Parallel Events In World History

1987 U.S. trade gap hit all-time high in October ($17.6 billions).	**1987** Nobel Peace Prize to Costa Rican President Oscar Arias for peace plan for Central America.	
1987 October stock market crash raised fears of unemployment in 1988.		
	1988 Supreme Court declared private club restrictions unconstitutional.	**1988** Palestinians rioted against Israeli control of Gaza; West Bank demanded self-government.
	1988 Benazio Bhutto became first Islamic woman to be Prime Minister of Pakistan.	**1989** Emperor Hirohito of Japan died at age 87, to be succeeded by his son.
1989 Space shuttle Atlantis launched a spacecraft on its trip to planet Jupiter.	**1989** Ronald Brown became first African-American chairman of the National Democratic Committee of the U.S.A.	**1989** Thousands of Chinese students took over Central Square in Peking to protest actions by government. Many killed by military police.
1989 Voyager II spacecraft submitted amazing report on planet Neptune.	**1989** Salman Rushdie's book *Satanic Verses* banned. The Ayatollah sentenced him and his publishers to death. Many protests by other countries; Rushdie forced into hiding.	**1989** Mikhail Gorbachev was named president of U.S.S.R. and announced he was in favor of a more open Russia.
1990 U.S. economy entered a recession.	**1990** Ellis Island restored.	**1990** East and West Germany reunited.
1990 Space shuttle Discovery carried Hubble telescope into space.	**1990** In the first authorized use of gene therapy, a four-year-old girl with a rare and deadly enzyme deficiency received genetically engineered cells to control her illness.	
		1991 Israel opened consulate in Moscow.
		1991 South African Schools integrated.
1991 Economy began to grow.		**1991** Mikhail Gorbachev resigned; U.S.S.R. broke up and constituent republics formed Commonwealth of Independent States.
		1991 Mt. Pinatubo in the Philippines erupted, causing global climate changes.
1992 Unemployment in the U.S.A. increased to over 7 percent, the worst in five and one-half years.	**1992** Miami emerged as center for Latin-American art.	**1992** A Serb campaign of "ethnic cleansing" against Muslims and Croats began in Sarajevo, Bosnia.
1992 Data from 1990 census challenged. Secretary of Commerce Mosbacher will release correct figures, upon which the allocation of representatives in Congress are based.	**1992** Film *JFK* stirred reaction that may lead to release of Warren Commission files relating to assassination of President John F. Kennedy.	
1992 Space Shuttle Atlantis launched its first spy satellite.		

Political and Governmental

Military & Special Events

American Foreign Relations

Political and Governmental	Military & Special Events	American Foreign Relations
1993 Clinton appointed Ruth Bader Ginsburg to the Supreme Court, replacing retiring Justice Byron R. White.		**1993** NAFTA and GATT approved by Congress.
1993 Bombing of World Trade Center in New York City.		
1994 Stephen G. Breyer replaced retiring Supreme Court Justice Harry A. Blackmun.	**1994** Clinton threatened armed force against Haiti if Aristide not allowed to return to power; Cedras stepped down.	
1995 Bombing of Alfred P. Murrah Federal Building in Oklahoma City.	**1995** Korean War Memorial opened.	**1995** Relations established with Hanoi.
1996 Bill Clinton re-elected. Republicans take over Congress; the Line Item Veto Bill gave the President power to cancel individual items in Appropriations Bills already signed; President signed Welfare Reform Bill.	**1996** U.N. sends arms inspection team to Iraq.	**1996** Provisions suspended on Anti-Cuba Bill passed by Congress (Helms-Burton Bill) which would permit American citizens whose property had been confiscated during Cuban Communist Revolution to sue in U.S. courts and would punish countries doing business with Cuba.
1997 Clinton and Gore inaugurated for a second term; by a narrow margin, Newt Gingrich re-elected Speaker of the House.	**1997** After dismissing U.N. nuclear arms inspection team, Iraq permits it to return; U.N. global warming conference held in Japan.	**1997** President Clinton urged the Senate to approve the nuclear test ban treaty; no action taken.
1998 The Supreme Court declared Line-Item Veto unconstitutional; the Supreme Court decided that the President, like any other American, may be sued in a civil case. The House impeached the President on charges of perjury and obstruction of justice and sent the case to the Senate, which later acquitted the President.	**1998** U.S. space shuttle "Discovery" flew mission with oldest astronaut aboard, Senator John Glenn of Ohio; India and Pakistan conducted underground nuclear tests.	**1998** Iraq again barred U.N. inspectors, claiming spying; U.S. threatened bombing. President Clinton visited China to discuss trade gap and human relations; the President was warmly received by Chinese people as he spoke to them on television.

Economic and Technological

Cultural and Intellectual

Parallel Events In World History

Economic and Technological	Cultural and Intellectual	Parallel Events In World History
1993 "Voicemail" became the norm in offices across the U.S.	**1993** Holocaust Memorial Museum opened in Washington, D.C.	
	1994 Education Act (Goals 2000)	**1994** First multiracial elections in South Africa; Nelson Mandela elected President.
	1994 Yitzhak Rabin, Shimon Peres, and Yasir Arafat won Nobel Peace Prize for their efforts in the Middle East.	**1994** Israel and Jordan signed peace treaty, formally ending 46 years of war.
		1994 Civil war reerupted in Rwanda.
		1994 Russia invaded Chechnya.
	1995 Rare book dealer discovered an apparently previously unknown poem by Edgar Allan Poe.	**1995** Major earthquake hit Japan.
		1995 Israeli Prime Minister Yitzhak Rabin was assassinated.
1996 Mergers in telecommunications industry at a record high. Scientists announce cloning of adult sheep.	**1996** U.S. Summit on Volunteerism held— General Colin Powell, heading the conference, urges more Americans to volunteer for public service.	**1996** Bosnia-Herzogovnia's Parliament meets for first time; Labour Party wins in British Parliamentary election; Blair succeeds John Major as Prime Minister.
1997 U.S. "Pathfinder" landed on Mars; exceptional photos sent home; Swiss banks offered restitution to Holocaust survivors.	**1997** Chinese dissident Wei arrived in U.S. to seek refuge.	**1997** NATO invited Poland, Hungary, and the Czech Republic to join; membership to take effect in 1999; Russia pulled out of Chechnya; Asian-Pacific Trade Conference held in Canada; Joblessness caused riots in France.
1998 Exxon and Mobile announced largest merger ever; Attorney General Janet Reno filed antitrust suit against Microsoft.	**1998** 50th anniversary of State of Israel. John Hume and David Trumble awarded Nobel Prize for Peace (Northern Ireland).	**1998** Netanyahu coalition collapsed; Israel set elections for Spring of 1999. In Cambodia, Khmer Rouge leaders surrendered; Yugoslav forces attacked Kosovo rebels; in Germany, Helmut Kohl, Chancellor for 18 years, defeated by Gerhard Schrader.

Immigration Update

I. The Immigration Reform and Control Act of 1986

This law, sometimes referred to as IRCA, took effect in November 1986, when it was signed by President Ronald Reagan. It included the legalization of undocumented aliens (without papers) if they entered the United States before 1982, as well as the legalization of farm workers who worked in the United States between May 1, 1985 and May 1, 1986. If such aliens applied for amnesty (pardon) between May 5, 1987 and May 4, 1988, and established that they

- lived in the United States continuously, without papers, since before January 1, 1982, and can prove such residence, and
- were never found guilty of a crime while here or outside the United States,

they were granted temporary resident status for 18 months. After that they had one year to apply for permanent residence status. But this residence is granted based on the original filing date of the temporary residence application. This results in the five-year waiting period.

Form I-698 is submitted by temporary residents for permanent status. Other aliens who worked in agricultural jobs (farms) were also eligible. After approval of temporary residence, they file Form I-90 to obtain permanent residence. (Sample forms are included in this book.) While the amnesty program is over, you may still be able to apply for legalization.

IRCA includes employer sanctions (penalties) for bosses who do not verify the status of all new workers they hire. If such employers do not complete Form I-9, they may have to pay a fine (a sum of money).

More information about eligibility can be obtained by writing to the district offices or the local offices listed in Unit 3. Mark your letter "Attention: Employer Relations Officer, Immigration and Naturalization Service."

II. The Immigration Act of 1990, P.L. 101-649

This law was passed by the 101st Congress and signed into law by President George Bush on November 29, 1990. Some of its provisions took effect on that date, but those with which we are concerned here, relating to family and job preferences, became effective October 1, 1991. October 14, 1991 was the date of the so-called "green-card lottery" in which the first 40,000 applications from 34 countries qualified for permanent residency.

Here we are concerned with some of the other provisions of P.L. 101-649 (P.L. stands for public law).

This law raises the number of entry visas that can be granted to family members of U.S. citizens or legal permanent residents of the United States. It also increases the number of visas that can be granted to certain categories of workers. While these changes will increase immigration to this country, preference will be given to immediate family members, professional workers, and migrants from Europe. Through this law, a whole new group of visas has been made available, some of which are highly selective. For example, persons who invest at least $1 million in a business here that will employ 10 or more American workers can apply for visas.

Provisions of this law that may affect you include:

1. The number of visas for immediate family members has been increased. This applies to citizens, permanent residents, and those who are in the process of establishing residence under the amnesty program. These persons may petition for entry of unmarried sons and daughters, and spouses. Citizens may petition for entry of married sons and married daughters, as well as for their brothers and sisters, provided the latter are at least 21 years old.

2. Workers sponsored by an employer in the United States may be given visas if:
   A. there is a shortage of workers in that line of work;
   B. the worker possesses specialized skills not held by unemployed citizens or legal residents;
   C. the worker has extraordinary ability, or
   D. is an outstanding professor, researcher, or manager;
   E. the applicant is a member of a profession and has an advanced degree;
   F. the worker is skilled and has more than two years' experience, or has graduated from college with a baccalaureate degree;
   G. the worker is unskilled with less than two years' experience. (There is a limit of 10,000 visas per year in this "little skills" class.)

Other benefits that exist under P.L. 101-649

1. 10,000 of those admitted as special workers can become residents and thus eligible for naturalization.
2. 10,000 investors can become permanent residents if they meet the qualifications (invest $1 million in a business here that employs at least 10 American workers).
3. 40,000 immigrants will be permitted from certain European countries, with 40% of the total going to Northern Ireland. In 1995, and later, 55,000 such immigrants will be admitted if they are from countries that underutilized their quotas.

If you have any questions about this law, it would be wise to check with one of the immigrant-serving agencies or an attorney who specializes in immigration law. Other parts of the Immigration Act of 1990 relating to deportation, bonding, antidiscrimination, and so on, while important, have not been included here since they are not directly related to the naturalization process.

Note the new words and phrases used in the text of this law:

spouse	husband or wife
underutilized	not fully used up
minors	children under 21 years of age
immediate relatives	minor children
	parents

Sample Completed Form N-400

When Anneta Quinones received her Application for Naturalization, she began to fill in the answers to the questions. She printed these answers and mailed the completed form, which you will find on the following pages, to 26 Federal Plaza, New York City.

As required, she sent two color photographs, taken within the last 30 days, and a completed Fingerprint Card. Of course, she did not send her Alien Registration Card, but she did send a money order for $95.

Mrs. Quinones arrived in New York on February 2, 1982 and was eligible for naturalization in 1987, but because of personal problems, did not apply until 1996.

Except for an absence of four weeks from the United States, Mrs. Quinones has lived continuously in New York State for many years. On Form N-400, she has printed all of the places where she lived and has included information about her trip out of the country.

At the present time, Mrs. Quinones is a nurse, but her limited English-speaking skills when she came to this country made it necessary for her to work as a cook in a restaurant for about two years. Information about her job record is included in item 4-B. At the present time she has 12 years' experience in a hospital in Brooklyn.

Aurora Quinones, her daughter, is 15 years old and a high school student. She will become a citizen when her mother is naturalized. The law states that a child admitted to the United States of America legally becomes a citizen if both parents are citizens. But if one parent is dead, or the parents are divorced, the child becomes a citizen when the custodial parent (legal guardian) does. Since the child in this case is under 18 years old, she will automatically become a citizen.

Mrs. Quinones works in a busy hospital, where the staff often call out "Annie" or "Quin" when they want her. She likes that, and has decided to change her name to Ann Quinn. If the judge agrees, there will be no charge for this change. The citizenship papers will be issued in the new name.

START HERE - Please Type or Print

Part 1.   Information about you.

Family Name **QUINONES**

Given Name **ANNETA**

Middle Initial

U.S. Mailing Address · Care of

Street Number and Name **1150 MIDWOOD ST.**   Apt. **# 3 B**

City **BROOKLYN**   County **KINGS**

State **NEW YORK**   ZIP Code **11225**

Date of Birth (month/day/year) **5-14-54**   Country of Birth **DOMINICAN REP.**

Social Security # **081-05-8153**   A # **21-241-841**

Part 2.   Basis for Eligibility (check one).

a.   ☒   I have been a permanent resident for at least five (5) years

b.   ☐   I have been a permanent resident for at least three (3) years and have been married to a United States Citizen for those three years.

c.   ☐   I am a permanent resident child of United States citizen parent(s).

d.   ☐   I am applying on the basis of qualifying military service in the Armed Forces of the U.S. and have attached completed Forms N-426 and G-325B.

e.   ☐   Other. (Please specify section of law) _____

Part 3.   Additional information about you.

Date you became a permanent resident (month/day/year) **2/2/82**

Port admitted with an immigrant visa or INS Office where granted adjustment of status. **NEW YORK, N.Y.**

Citizenship **DOMINICAN**

Name on alien registration card (if different than in Part 1) _____

Other names used since you became a permanent resident (including maiden name) **ANNETA ROSA**

Sex   ☐ Male   ☒ Female   Height **5'3"**

Marital Status: ☐ Single   ☐ Married   ☐ Divorced   ☒ Widowed

Can you speak, read and write English?   ☐ No   ☒ Yes.

Absences from the U.S.:

Have you been absent from the U.S. since becoming a permanent resident?   ☐ No   ☒ Yes.

If you answered "Yes", complete the following. Begin with your most recent absence. If you need more room to explain the reason for an absence or to list more trips, continue on separate paper.

Date left U.S.	Date returned	Did absence last 6 months or more?	Destination	Reason for trip
7/1/85	**8/30/85**	☐ Yes ☒ No	**DOMINICAN**	**ILLNESS**
		☐ Yes ☐ No	**REPUBLIC**	**OF MOTHER**
		☐ Yes ☐ No		
		☐ Yes ☐ No		
		☐ Yes ☐ No		
		☐ Yes ☐ No		

Form N-400 (Rev. 07/17/91)N   *Continued on back.*

FOR INS USE ONLY

Returned	Receipt
Resubmitted	
Reloc Sent	
Reloc Rec'd	
☐ Applicant Interviewed	

At interview

☐ request naturalization ceremony at court

Remarks

Action

To Be Completed by
Attorney or Representative, if any

☐ Fill in box if G-28 is attached to represent the applicant

VOLAG#

ATTY State License #

Figure 28

Part 4. Information about your residences and employment.

A. List your addresses during the last five (5) years or since you became a permanent resident, whichever is less. Begin with your current address. If you need more space, continue on separate paper:

Street Number and Name, City, State, Country, and Zip Code	Dates (month/day/year) From	To
1150 MIDWOOD ST. BROOKLYN, N.Y. KINGS 11225	JAN 15 1984	PRESENT
380 W. 83 ST. NEW YORK, NY NY 10025	FEB 2 1982	JAN 15 1984

B. List your employers during the last five (5) years. List your present or most recent employer first. If none, write "None". If you need more space, continue on separate paper.

Employer's Name	Employer's Address Street Name and Number - City, State and ZIP Code	Dates Employed (month/day/year) From	To	Occupation/position
KINGS COUNTY HOSPITAL	CLARKSON AVE. BKLYN N.Y. 11225	JAN 1 1984	PRESENT	PRACTICAL NURSE
CAFE AMERICA	285 BWAY. N.Y. N.Y. 10003	MAR 1 1982	12/31/83	COOK

Part 5. Information about your marital history.

A. Total number of times you have been married **ONE**. If you are now married, complete the following regarding your husband or wife.

Family name N/A	Given name N/A	Middle initial N/A

Address N/A

Date of birth (month/day/year) N/A	Country of birth N/A	Citizenship N/A
Social Security# N/A	A# (if applicable) N/A	Immigration status (If not a U.S. citizen) N/A

Naturalization (If applicable) (month/day/year) N/A   Place (City, State) N/A

If you have ever previously been married or if your current spouse has been previously married, please provide the following on separate paper: Name of prior spouse, date of marriage, date marriage ended, how marriage ended and immigration status of prior spouse.

Part 6. Information about your children.

B. Total Number of Children **ONE**   Complete the following information for each of your children. If the child lives with you, state "with me" in the address column; otherwise give city/state/country of child's current residence. If deceased, write "deceased" in the address column. If you need more space, continue on separate paper.

Full name of child	Date of birth	Country of birth	Citizenship	A - Number	Address
AURORA QUINONES	6-29-88	DOM.REP.	DOMINICAN		WITH ME

Form N-400 (Rev 07/17/91)N   *Continued on next page*

Figure 28 (cont.)

Part 7. Additional eligibility factors.

Please answer each of the following questions. If your answer is **"Yes"**, explain on a separate paper.

1. Are you now, or have you ever been a member of, or in any way connected or associated with the Communist Party, or ever knowingly aided or supported the Communist Party directly, or indirectly through another organization, group or person, or ever advocated, taught, believed in, or knowingly supported or furthered the interests of communism? ☐ Yes ☒ No

2. During the period March 23, 1933 to May 8, 1945, did you serve in, or were you in any way affiliated with, either directly or indirectly, any military unit, paramilitary unit, police unit, self-defense unit, vigilante unit, citizen unit of the Nazi party or SS, government agency or office, extermination camp, concentration camp, prisoner of war camp, prison, labor camp, detention camp or transit camp, under the control or affiliated with:
    a. The Nazi Government of Germany? ☐ Yes ☒ No
    b. Any government in any area occupied by, allied with, or established with the assistance or cooperation of, the Nazi Government of Germany? ☐ Yes ☒ No

3. Have you at any time, anywhere, ever ordered, incited, assisted, or otherwise participated in the persecution of any person because of race, religion, national origin, or political opinion? ☐ Yes ☒ No

4. Have you ever left the United States to avoid being drafted into the U.S. Armed Forces? ☐ Yes ☒ No

5. Have you ever failed to comply with Selective Service laws? ☐ Yes ☒ No
    If you have registered under the Selective Service laws, complete the following information:
    Selective Service Number: _____ Date Registered: _____
    If you registered before 1978, also provide the following:
    Local Board Number: _____ Classification: _____

6. Did you ever apply for exemption from military service because of alienage, conscientious objections or other reasons? ☐ Yes ☒ No

7. Have you ever deserted from the military, air or naval forces of the United States? ☐ Yes ☒ No

8. Since becoming a permanent resident, have you ever failed to file a federal income tax return? ☐ Yes ☒ No

9. Since becoming a permanent resident, have you filed a federal income tax return as a nonresident or failed to file a federal return because you considered yourself to be a nonresident? ☐ Yes ☒ No

10 Are deportation proceedings pending against you, or have you ever been deported, or ordered deported, or have you ever applied for suspension of deportation? ☐ Yes ☒ No

11. Have you ever claimed in writing, or in any way, to be a United States citizen? ☐ Yes ☒ No

12. Have you ever:
    a. been a habitual drunkard? ☐ Yes ☒ No
    b. advocated or practiced polygamy? ☐ Yes ☒ No
    c. been a prostitute or procured anyone for prostitution? ☐ Yes ☒ No
    d. knowingly and for gain helped any alien to enter the U.S. illegally? ☐ Yes ☒ No
    e. been an illicit trafficker in narcotic drugs or marijuana? ☐ Yes ☒ No
    f. received income from illegal gambling? ☐ Yes ☒ No
    g. given false testimony for the purpose of obtaining any immigration benefit? ☐ Yes ☒ No

13. Have you ever been declared legally incompetent or have you ever been confined as a patient in a mental institution? ☐ Yes ☒ No

14. Were you born with, or have you acquired in same way, any title or order of nobility in any foreign State? ☐ Yes ☒ No

15. Have you ever:
    a. knowingly committed any crime for which you have not been arrested? ☐ Yes ☒ No
    b. been arrested, cited, charged, indicted, convicted, fined or imprisoned for breaking or violating any law or ordinance excluding traffic regulations? ☐ Yes ☒ No

(If you answer yes to 15 , in your explanation give the following information for each incident or occurrence the **city**, **state**, and **country**, where the offense took place, the **date** and **nature** of the offense, and the **outcome** or **disposition** of the case).

Part 8. Allegiance to the U.S.

If your answer to any of the following questions is **"NO"**, attach a full explanation:

1. Do you believe in the Constitution and form of government of the U.S.? ☒ Yes ☐ No
2. Are you willing to take the full Oath of Allegiance to the U.S.? (see instructions) ☒ Yes ☐ No
3. If the law requires it, are you willing to bear arms on behalf of the U.S.? ☒ Yes ☐ No
4. If the law requires it, are you willing to perform noncombatant services in the Armed Forces of the U.S.? ☒ Yes ☐ No
5. If the law requires it, are you willing to perform work of national importance under civilian direction? ☒ Yes ☐ No

Form N-400 (Rev. 07/17/91)N

Continued on back

Figure 28 (cont.)

Part 9. Memberships and organizations.

A. List your present and past membership in or affiliation with every organization, association, fund, foundation, party, club, society, or similar group in the United States or in any other place. Include any military service in this part. If none, write "none". Include the name of organization, location, dates of membership and the nature of the organization. If additional space is needed, use separate paper.

HOSPITAL EMPLOYEES UNION BROOKLYN, NY   JAN. 1984 - PRESENT

Part 10. Complete only if you checked block " C " in Part 2.

How many of your parents are U.S. citizens? ☐ One   ☐ Both   (Give the following about one U.S. citizen parent:)

Family Name	Given Name	Middle Name

Address

Basis for citizenship:	Relationship to you (check one):	☐ natural parent	☐ adoptive parent
☐ Birth			
☐ Naturalization Cert. No.		☐ parent of child legitimated after birth	

If adopted or legitimated after birth, give date of adoption or, legitimation: *(month/day/year)* _____

Does this parent have legal custody of you?   ☐ Yes   ☐ No

(Attach a copy of relating evidence to establish that you are the child of this U.S. citizen and evidence of this parent's citizenship.)

Part 11. Signature. *(Read the information on penalties in the instructions before completing this section).*

I certify or, if outside the United States, I swear or affirm, under penalty of perjury under the laws of the United States of America that this application, and the evidence submitted with it, is all true and correct. I authorize the release of any information from my records which the Immigration and Naturalization Service needs to determine eligibility for the benefit I am seeking.

Signature   Date

Anneta R. Quinones   *August 15, 1996*

Please Note: If you do not completely fill out this form, or fail to submit required documents listed in the instructions, you may not be found eligible for naturalization and this application may be denied.

Part 12. Signature of person preparing form if other than above. *(Sign below)*

I declare that I prepared this application at the request of the above person and it is based on all information of which I have knowledge.

Signature   Print Your Name   Date

Firm Name and Address

DO NOT COMPLETE THE FOLLOWING UNTIL INSTRUCTED TO DO SO AT THE INTERVIEW

I swear that I know the contents of this application, and supplemental pages 1 through_____, that the corrections , numbered 1 through_____, were made at my request, and that this amended application, is true to the best of my knowledge and belief.

Subscribed and sworn to before me by the applicant.

_____
(Examiner's Signature)   Date

_____
(Complete and true signature of applicant)

Word List

WORD	MEANING
A abbreviation	a shortened form of a word
ability	knowledge and skill needed to do something
abolished	put an end to; did away with
abridge	to make shorter; to lessen
accept	to receive
active	moving; doing one's work, doing things
adjourn	to put off to a later time
administer	to direct or to give
admitted	given the right to enter
adopted	accepted; agreed to; taken as one's own
adult	full-grown; matured
advantage	benefit
advise	inform; tell
afford	be able to spend money for something
agency	a company or office or organization in business to act for another's benefit
agree	to say "yes"; to have the same opinion
agriculture	the science of farming land
alien	person from a foreign country; person not yet a citizen
amnesty	a pardon
allegiance	loyalty
allow	permit
amendment	a change or an addition to a constitution or law
amount	total sum
annexation	uniting; adding to

WORD	MEANING
anthem	a song or hymn of praise or allegiance
appeal	to take a question from a lower to a higher authority
appeared	was seen; seemed to be
applicant	a person who applies for something
application	a form used to make a request
apply	to ask for something; to let people know you want something
appointed	named to take a job or office
apportion	to make a division
approve	agree to; to think well of; to say "yes"
area	amount of land; level space
argue	discuss; give reasons in support of ideas
arrive	to reach a place; come
assemble	meet together for a common purpose
assistance	help; aid
attorney	a person acting for another person at law
avoid	to keep away from

B

WORD	MEANING
backbone	the most important part
background	the result of training, experience, education
balance	to make equal in value; to make even
base	foundation
basic	serving as a starting point
basis	the main part; supporting element
belief	faith; trust
belongings	things a person owns
benefit	anything that is for the good of a person or thing; money paid to a person
bill	a suggested law proposed by a lawmaker
Bill of Rights	the first ten Amendments to the Constitution
borrow	to get something from another person with the understanding that it must be returned
boundary	the line, real or imaginary, that shows where a piece of land ends
brief	short

C

WORD	MEANING
cabinet	group of advisers to the President
candidate	person who runs for office
capital	city where the government is located
Capitol	the building in which the U.S. Congress meets
cattle	farm animals; livestock
cause	the thing a person fights for; reason
celebrate	to recognize and honor, as a holiday
census	an official count of people
center	a middle point; place where people meet

WORD	MEANING
certificate	written statement of proof of some fact
character (good)	a good name or a reputation for being responsible and moral
charge	ask as a price; fee
cheaper	costing less
check	to control; hold back; restrain
chief executive	the highest officer of government
choice	a thing preferred; selection
choose	decide to take; pick out
circular	a printed paper containing information
citizen	a person having full rights in the place where he/she lives
civil	relating to private rights; having to do with government service
civil service	government work
claim	ask for as a right
classified ads	short advertisements listed by alphabet in a newspaper
colonies	settlements in a new land
comfort	something that makes life easier
commerce	trade or business
commissions	small groups of people working for a government
communication	the giving of information
community	city or town; neighborhood
compare	to show how things are alike or different
compensation	payment for work done or for some other purpose
completes	finishes
comply	obey
concern	anxiety; interest
condition	how a person or thing is
conduct	manage; carry on
Congress	the main lawmaking body of the United States
conquest	gained by force
consent	to agree; to say "yes"
considers	thinks about; makes allowance for
Constitution	basic law of the United States
contain	to hold; to have; include
continuous	without stopping
contributions	things given to others; gifts
convenience	anything that adds to one's comfort
convention	a meeting for some purpose
conversation	informal talk
costly	expensive; costing a great deal of money
courage	bravery
create	make

WORD	MEANING
criminal	having to do with a wrongful act against society
crude	rough; not pure

D

debate	argument about issues; to take sides in a discussion
debt	something owed by one person to another or others
decide	settle a question
declaration	a public statement
Declaration of Independence	a public statement by which the Continental Congress in 1776 said that the 13 colonies were free from Great Britain
Declaration of Intention	a legal paper in which an alien says that he/she intends to become a citizen
declare	to make known openly
defeated	beaten; to win victory over
defense	protection from others
delegate	a person sent to speak or act for others; a representative
democracy	government of, by, and for the people
department	a division or branch of governmental administration
dependent	person needing support—a husband or wife, child, etc.
deposits	material laid down by natural means
deprive	to withhold something from
descendants	children, grandchildren, great-grandchildren
desert	a region without water
destroyed	broken to pieces; ruined; spoiled
difficult	not easy
diploma	paper that says a person has graduated from a school
disabled	unable to do what most people do; unable to work
disagreement	difference of opinion; quarrel; dispute
discovered	found
discuss	to talk over
dispute	a heated argument
dissatisfaction	not giving pleasure
dissent	to disagree
district	the part of a state that a congressman represents
document	written proof
domestic	having to do with our own country; relating to household or family
domestic workers	people who do housework for a living
drug	something taken into the body to help a person get well
due process of law	a limit on the actions of government

WORD	MEANING
E earn	to make money by working
education	instruction
effect	(used with "in") operational
elected	chosen by the voters
eligible/eligibility	qualified for something; fit to be chosen
employer	the person or company for whom you work
employment	work
energy	power, such as electricity or heat
enforce	make people do something; to compel
enjoy	to like; to have the benefit of something
equality	sameness in importance; being equal
established	started; set up; founded
examination	test
examiner	person who examines or questions another person
exception	a situation that doesn't follow the general rule
exciting	giving great joy; feeling stirred up
executive	person who runs things; the boss; executive branch of government that enforces law
exist	to live
expensive	costly
experience	what one has done in the past; anything seen, done, or lived through
export	to send to foreign countries
express	say; write; let people know how you feel or think
extended	spread; reached out; made longer
F factories	places where things are made
fame	being well known
federation	a group in which members are united but keep self-government
fee	charge for services or privileges; cost
file	to submit an application or a petition
finally	at the end; at last
fingerprint	mark of a finger that can be used to identify someone
flows	runs like water
formed	organized; developed; came together
former	the one before; the first
founded	started; built for the first time
freedom	not under control by others; to be able to do as one wants
friendly	kindly
function	duty or job
furnished	having furniture; put in what was needed

WORD	MEANING
G general	usual; belonging to all
general election	a time when people may vote for any candidate
government	a system of ruling people
graduate	to complete a course of study in a school or college
grant	to give
guarantee	a promise to do something; pledge; stand behind
H hardships	troubles
headed	led by
hemisphere	half of the world
highway	main road
hires	employs; gives a job to
honor	to show respect
House of Representatives	the lower house of the U.S. Congress
housing project	group of houses or apartments in one location
I immigrant	a newcomer to a country
immunity	freedom from something
important	meaning much; worthwhile
impress	to make someone remember you; influence
improve	to grow better
include	to form or be a part of something
increase	become larger
independent	free from control by others
individual	a person
industrial centers	places where there are many factories
ineligible	not qualified
informal	not according to rule; without ceremony; relaxed
information	news; knowledge; facts you learn
informed	to know about; to have knowledge of
institution	organization of a public nature
insures	protects; makes certain; guarantees
intelligence	mental power or ability
intelligent	having knowledge; skilled; able to learn quickly
interesting	holds one's attention
interfere	to enter into the affairs of others; meddle; to clash
interpret	to help people to understand
interpreter	a person who explains in one language something that was said in a different language
interview	conversation between an employer and a person who is asking for a job
invaded	entered with the purpose of taking possession
invented	made for the first time
irrigate	to bring water to crops; to water
issue	a problem needing a decision

WORD	MEANING
J judicial	having to do with courts and judges and interpreting the laws
jurisdiction	control
jury	a group of people sworn to hear the evidence and give a decision in a case
K knowledge	information; news; facts
L landlord	person who owns an apartment house or other rental property
lawfully	according to the law
lease	an agreement to rent a house or apartment
legal	correct according to law; having to do with law
legislation	making and passing laws
legislative	having to do with making laws
legislature	lawmaking body
lending	allowing the use of something for a while
level	even
librarian	person in charge of a library
library	a building containing a collection of books; also a collection of books
license	to authorize by legal permit
listed	written in order
living	being alive
local	nearby; in your own neighborhood or city
located	in; in a certain place
loyal	true to one's friends or country
M majority	most; more than half of those voting
manufacture	to make, usually in a factory
marital	having to do with being married
member	a person who is part of a group of people
mine	a pit from which coal or ore is dug
minimum	the smallest number or amount
miracle	a remarkable thing or event
mode	the way in which something is done
moral	having to do with right and wrong
motor vehicle	car, automobile, or truck
mourned	felt sad
N narrow	limited; not wide
native-born	born in the country where a person lives
naturalization hearing	an examination of an applicant for citizenship
naturalized	admitted to citizenship
necessary	needed; essential

WORD	MEANING
needy	poor; not having enough to live on
neighbor	person living near another person
neighborhood	place where people live near one another; community
newcomer	person in this country for a short time; an alien
nominate	to name or propose for office
nominee	a person named as a candidate for office
notice	to see; a written or printed sign giving information or warning; announcement

O

WORD	MEANING
oath	solemn promise of the truth of a statement
occupation	the kind of work a person does
official	officer holding a government job; formal
operate	to work; to act
opinion	a particular judgment or belief; what one thinks
opportunity	chance to do or get something
ore	rock, sand, or dirt having some metal in it
organize	get people together for a purpose; to plan

P

WORD	MEANING
pamphlet	little booklet
participate	to take part or share in
pension	regular payment of living expenses to person who has retired
permanent	steady; lasting; fixed
permit	allow
persecute	to treat someone cruelly because of his or her beliefs
persecution	cruel treatment of a person because of one's beliefs
petition	a formal written request
physical	having to do with the body
Pilgrims	settlers who came from England and founded the colony of Plymouth in 1620
Pledge of Allegiance	a formal statement of loyalty to the government
political opinion	a general thought on what is going on in government
politician	a person who works for a political party
politics	affairs of government; management of political affairs
polls	places where people vote
population	people; the number of people in a place
posterity	people who will live in the future
postmaster	person in charge of a post office
poultry	chickens, turkeys, geese, ducks
power	strong nation; strength; might; force
preamble	the opening part of a statement
precious	dear; of great value
prefer	to like one thing better than another; to choose; to decide in favor or

WORD	MEANING
prescription	written order to a druggist telling him to make a certain medicine
preserve	to keep
prey	to attack; a victim, or one who is helpless under attack
primary election	a time when people nominate, rather than elect, a candidate
principal	main; most important; chief
private	belonging to or concerning an individual; personal; one's own; not public
privately-owned	owned by individuals, rather than a community
privilege	benefit or advantage
problems	questions
process	series of actions
proclamation	an official public announcement or notice; official publication
produce	to make or manufacture; grow
products	things made or grown for use
professional	relating to a job requiring special education
prohibits	does not permit; forbids
proper	right; correct
protection	providing safety; keeping a person or thing from being harmed
proud	thinking well of one's self
provides	gives; makes possible
public	belonging to the people of a community, state, or nation; not private
public housing projects	a group of houses built by the city, state, or federal government
public office	a position in the service of a nation, state, or city
purposes	reasons for doing something
Q qualification	requirement
R ratify	to approve
reasons	explanations
receipt	written statement that someone has received something
record	thing written or kept for future use
references	letters from employers saying how good a worker a person is
refineries	places where raw materials are made ready for use
refugee	a person who leaves a country because of persecution
regarding	about

WORD	MEANING
region	area; section of a country or state
register	have one's name written into a list of people who can take a job or can vote
regularly	at certain, expected times
relatives	people in one's own family
religious	relating to faith and worship
remind	to tell again
rent	to pay for the use of land, home, property; the money paid for such use
represent	to speak and work for a person or a group of people
representative	a person chosen to act for another; delegate
republic	a system of representative government
requirement	something needed
residence	place where a person lives
resource	any supply that will meet a need
respect	show honor
responsibility	a task; a debt; a duty
retire	give up a job or office; stop working
right	something to which one has a just claim; any power or privilege given a person by law, custom, etc.
rivals	persons who are opponents
rule	guide; govern; control

S

WORD	MEANING
sanitation	keeping things clean for health reasons
secret	known only to oneself
security	safety; financial comfort
seeking	looking for
select	choose
self-educated	taught by oneself
Senate	the upper house of the U.S. Congress
separate	keep apart
separation of powers	duties that have no connection with each other
service	a convenience; a useful thing to be done or given; a helpful act
service trades	jobs that make other people more comfortable
settle	set up a home; live
share	to use and enjoy together
shortage	too small a number or amount; not enough
shorthand	writing by symbols
skill	great ability
slavery	the owning or keeping of slaves
slogan	a group of words making the purpose of something clear
Social Security	a federal plan to take care of workers in their old age
solved	figured out; found the answer

WORD	MEANING
source	place where something comes from
specialized	different; unusual; requiring special training
spouse	wife or husband
standard of living	way of living; things needed and used in order to live in a certain way
"Star-Spangled Banner"	the national anthem of the U.S.A.
stationery	articles such as paper, pens, ink, pencils, etc.
stenography	writing in shorthand
strange	not known or heard of before
strength	ability; force; power
structure	a framework, a building
struggle	battle; fight
suffrage	the right to vote
suggests	hints; mentions
supply	to give, provide, or fill
supreme	highest in importance
surveyor	person who measures and marks land
survived	lived after others died
sworn	bound by oath
symbol	an object that stands for something else
system of checks and balances	each branch of government has powers that to some degree control the powers of others

T

WORD	MEANING
tenant	person who rents an apartment, house, etc. from another or from a landlord
territory	land; region; land belonging to a government
textiles	woven cloth
trade	business; work one does
trained	taught; made ready and able to do something
traitor	person who works against his own country
tranquility	condition of being calm, peaceful, or quiet
treasury	the country's money
treaty	agreement between nations
tuition	money paid to a school in order to attend it
type	kind; sort; typewrite

U

WORD	MEANING
unalienable	cannot be taken away or lessened
unconstitutional	not according to the Constitution or law
undocumented	without legal documents
uneducated	not trained; unskilled
union	people joined together for a common purpose
unity	being together; being or acting as one
unusual	not common; rare
uphold	to support
urban	relating to a city or town

WORD	MEANING
V vacancy	an empty apartment, house, or room that can be rented; a job that is open
valid	having force in law
veto	refuse to allow a bill to become a law by not signing it
vocational	having to do with trades
void	not in force
W want	need; something needed
wealth	riches; land; resources; money
welcome	greeting
wise	to have great understanding of persons, conditions, and situations
witnesses	persons who give testimony and evidence
wonder	think about; want to know why
worship	pray to; pay honor and respect to

Answer Key

Pretest

PAGE 3

1–6. You must answer these yourself since they pertain to individual matters.

7. 50

8. Democracy.

9. Congress.

10. Legislative, executive, judicial.

11. Constitution.

12. Supreme Court.

13. President.

14. Governor.

15. Vote.

16. Red, white, and blue.

17. Red for courage, white for truth, blue for honor.

18. 13

19. 50

20. "Star-Spangled Banner"

Citizenship

REVIEW   PAGE 12

1–5. See Word List, page 197.

6. a. Alien.

b. Easy.

7. Easy.

8. A citizen.

9. Being part of the government of the United States is a benefit of citizenship.

10. Being able to vote is a citizen's right.

REVIEW   PAGE 14

1–8. See Word List, page 197.

9. In a U.S. courtroom.

10. The Oath of Allegiance is a pledge of loyalty to the United States.

11. To live here and to be part of the country.

12. Yes.

13. No.

REVIEW   PAGE 15

1. Moving from one place to another.
2. About 40 million.
3. The Immigration Act of 1990.
4. 1899.
5. 1600s.

REVIEW   PAGE 17

1–6. See Word List, page 197.
7. The Constitution.
8. 27
9. The Fourteenth Amendment.
10. They are the rights to life, liberty, and property. No matter where I live, these rights cannot be taken away without due process of law.
11. Liberty.

QUIZ   PAGE 20

1–7. See Word List, page 197.
8. No.
9. To obey the laws, to know what is going on, to vote, to serve on a jury.
10. To have a voice in government.
11. To make it possible for persons to have a fair trial.
12. To be loyal to the Constitution and government, to obey the laws, to vote, to defend the country, to serve on a jury.

QUIZ   PAGE 21

1. You must be 18 years or older.
2. No.
3. Page 187.
4. Marriage to a citizen.
5. No.

Step 3—Serious Study

PRACTICE TEST   PAGE 68

1. Eighteen years old.
2. Yes.
3. You must have resided in this country for five years.* In these five years, you must have been physically present at least 30 months, and you must have resided for at least six months in the state from which you are filing.
4–5. Yes, *unless* you have a physical or developmental disability or a mental impairment that prevents you, or you are over 50 years old and have lived in the United States 20 or more years, or you are over 55 years old and have lived in the United States for 15 or more years.
6. Yes.
7. Yes.
8. Yes.
9. Yes.

---

*A husband or wife of an American citizen may apply for naturalization after three rather than five years' residence, provided that the husband and wife were actually living together during that time.

NOTE: *A husband and wife who file for naturalization must do so separately. A husband's naturalization does not make his wife a citizen, or vice versa. Children born abroad may become citizens if they are under 16 years of age at the time their parents are naturalized.*

10. Yes. If you have a physical or developmental disability or a mental impairment, you may be exempt from this requirement.

11. The first step in the naturalization process is to obtain an Application for Naturalization (Form N-400) from the Immigration and Naturalization Service. You can get Form N-400 and the other papers that you need by telephoning the INS Forms Line at 1-800-870-3676.

12. It means that you were admitted to this country for permanent residence and that you have a green card.

13. Your name must be spelled exactly as it appears on your Permanent Resident Card so that the records of your lawful admission can be verified. Your address must be exactly right so that you receive promptly any papers mailed to you. Any errors will cause a delay in your becoming a citizen.

14. You may change your name if the judge of the immigration court approves your request.

15. Even though a Declaration of Intention (formerly called the First Paper) is not required for citizenship, an employer may wish to see that you are serious about becoming a citizen. Also, for some licenses, it is necessary to have this form.

16. *Employment*—Although immigrants are entitled to work in the United States, they are excluded from holding jobs with the federal government and from some local or state government jobs (those involving peacekeeping).

    Voting—Only citizens can vote.

    Public office—Only citizens can run for public office.

17. A permanent resident.

18. Yes. They are entitled to live here permanently, to travel, to receive most types of public assistance, to work, and to benefit from the full protection of our laws.

19. No. People in the United States with nonimmigrant, or temporary, visas—that is, tourists, students, exchange visitors, and so on—cannot become citizens.

20. No. Although voting is one of the most important benefits of citizenship and every voter must be a citizen, not all citizens exercise this right.

21. Any time after the required residence has been established, usually five years after entering the country for permanent residence or three years for persons married to U.S. citizens.

22. Yes. The Immigration and Naturalization Service has the right to make a neighborhood check or an investigation of the applicant's work site or sites for the five years before filing to determine the character and fitness of the applicant.

23. Yes. Some time after Form N-400 is filed, the applicant will be called to the naturalization interview. There, the naturalization examiner will ask several questions about our government and history.

24. If the applicant is prepared, this examination will be easy. Being prepared means learning as much as you can from this book about government, history, and the meaning of citizenship. It also means finding out about the people who represent you and wanting to make your vote count when you become a citizen.

25. The most important thing to do is to be on time, or a little early, for the appointment. Dress conservatively. In fact, dress as though you were going to a job interview. Bring your Permanent Resident Card. And remember, there is nothing to be nervous about!

26–31. You must look this information up yourself since it pertains to individual matters.

REVIEW   PAGE 80

1. Constitution.
2. Ratified.
3. 13
4. Colonies.
5. Americans.
6. They would have to present the idea to a member of Congress who could introduce it as a bill. If it is passed by a two-thirds vote in both houses, it could be sent to the 50 states for ratification. Three-quarters of the state legislatures would have to ratify before it could become part of the Constitution.

REVIEW   PAGE 87

1–8. See Word List, page 197.
9. Checks and balances, separation of powers.
10. Legislative, Senate, House of Representatives.
11. Executive.
12. Vice president.
13. Judicial, interprets.

REVIEW   PAGE 90

1–6. See Word List, page 197.
7. One represents the 50 states, the other, the people of the state.
8. No.
9. January 3.
10. When members vote to adjourn, or close, the session.
11. Read page 91.
12. The committee system was devised to make the work of Congress easier.

REVIEW   PAGE 96

1–9. See Word List, page 197.
10. To carry out the laws.
11. Many responsibilities.

12. The cabinet.
13. No.
14. He takes the Presidential Oath of Office at his inauguration.

REVIEW   PAGE 98

1–4. See Word List, page 197.
5. To interpret the laws.
6. Supreme Court.
7. Eight associate justices and one chief justice are all appointed by the president.
8. William Rehnquist.
9. Yes.
10. c
11. c
12. a
13. d

REVIEW   PAGE 100

1–8. See Word List, page 197.
9. The Tenth Amendment provides this right.

REVIEW   PAGE 105

1–6. See Word List, page 197.
7. Representation.
8. Unalienable.
9. The United States.
10. Traitors, traitor.
11. Dissatisfaction.

REVIEW   PAGE 108

1–5. See Word List, page 197.
6. *because* these are the colors of the flag.
7. *because* there were 13 states in the beginning.
8. *because* there are 50 states today.
9. *because* they were part of Britain.
10. *because* the flag was adopted on that date in 1777.

REVIEW PAGE 109

1. Christopher Columbus, 1492.
2. 1607, Jamestown, Virginia.
3. The Pilgrims.
4. England.
5. Taxes imposed on people who have no voice in the government.
6. July 4, 1776.
7. July 4, 1776.
8. George Washington.
9. Abraham Lincoln was president during the Civil War. He preserved the Union.
10. The Emancipation Proclamation was a document issued by Abraham Lincoln that freed the slaves in the South.
11. A democracy or a republic.
12. The Constitution.
13. 1789.
14. Yes, by amendments, 27 times.
15. Legislative, executive, and judicial.
16. Congress.
17. The Supreme Court.
18. Yes. There are state and local governments.
19. There are 50 states.
20. Red, white, and blue. The red is for courage, the white for truth, and the blue is for honor.
21. The "Star-Spangled Banner."
22. Abraham Lincoln, 1861–1865.
23. It ceases to be in effect.
24. He can veto the bill.
25. Yes, by a two-thirds vote of the Congress.

Appendix   American English Practice

REVIEW PAGE 125

1. used to
2. have time
3. out of the question
4. lay off
5. a little while
6. write away
7. looking forward
8. heard from
9. Bear in mind
10. breakdown

Index

1960s, 176–178
1970s, 178–180
1980s, 180–182
1990s, 182–185

A

Adjourn, 90
Alien, 9, 11
Alien Registration Receipt Card, 55
Amendment, 17
Amendments to Constitution, 83–84,
    143–147
American Revolution and Confederation
    (1763–1789), 154–156
Anthem, 107
Attorney general, 95

B

Bill becomes a law, 90–91
Bill of Rights, 80, 82, 86
Bush, George, 13

C

Cabinet members, 92, 95
Checks and balances, 87, 89
Chief executive, 94
Chief justice of the Supreme Court, 94
Citizens
    description of, 11–12
    responsibilities of, 19–20

Citizenship, 11
    eligibility for, 25–26
    filling out forms, 57–63
    forms and fees for, 28–55
    review of steps to, 115
Civil War, 162
Cold War period, 172–176
Common Sense (Paine), 104
Congress, 87
Conservative Era (1877–1901), 164–166
Conservative Republican Era (1921–1933),
    170–171
Constitution of the United States, 17, 80–84
    text of, 137–142
Continuous residence, 54
Court system, 96, 98

D

Declaration of Independence, 104–105
    text of, 133–135
Declaration of Intending Citizen, 54
Declaration of Intention, 54
Delegated powers, 102
Democracy, 19, 78
Dissent, 98

E

Early national period (1789–1828),
    156–159
Educational requirements, 77–118

English practice
   idiomatic expressions, 121–125
   pronunciation, 127–128
Exceptions to citizenship requirements, 21
Executive branch, 87, 92
Exploration and colonization period (to 1763), 150–154

F

Federal government, 87–99, 103, 131–132
Federation, 78
Fees, 27–28
Fifth Amendment, 86
Final test, 109–111
Flag, 8, 107–108
Flag Day, 107
Form 9003, 41
Form G-325A (Biographic Information), 42
Form I-817 (Application for Voluntary Departure Under the Family Unity Program), 50–53
Form I-485 (Application to Register Permanent Residence or Adjust Status), 35–38
Form I-90 (Application to Replace Alien Registration Card), 45–46
Form I-130 (Petition for Alien Relative), 47–49
Form I-485 Supplement A, 39–40
Form N-400 (Application for Naturalization), 31–34
   completed sample, 191–195
   filling out, 59–63
Form N-565 (Application for Replacement Naturalization/Citizenship Document), 43–44
Form N-300 (Application to File Declaration of Intention), 29–30
Forms, 29–54
   filling out, 57–63
   where to send, 58–59
Fourteenth Amendment, 17, 86

G

Good moral character, 71–72
Government, 78, 85, 101 See also Federal government; Local government; State government
Green card, 55

H

History of United States, 148–185
Holidays, 129

I

Idiomatic expressions, 121–125
Immigrants, 13, 16
Immigration, 15
Immigration Act of 1990, 13, 15, 188–189
Immigration and Nationality Act, 25
Immigration and Naturalization Service (INS), 9
Immigration Reform and Control Act (1986), 13, 15, 54, 75, 187–188

J

Jacksonian Democracy (1828–1850), 160–161
Jefferson, Thomas, 104
Judicial branch, 87, 96–97

K

Kennedy, John F., 13

L

Law, 87–88, 91–92
Legislative branch, 87
Liberty Bell, 106
Lincoln, Abraham, 95
Local government, 100
   questions regarding, 5–6
Lost papers, 55

N

Naturalization, 9, 13
   educational requirements for, 77–118
   requirements for, 68–71, 73
Naturalization interview, 113–114
New Deal (1933–1939), 172

O

Oath of Allegiance, 13, 107, 115

P

Paine, Thomas, 104
Pledge of Allegiance, 107
President of United States, 92–95
Pretest, 3–6
Probability Questions, 64–66, 116–117
Progress test
   reading practice
      good moral character, 71–72
      Immigration Reform and Control Act, 75
      who can be naturalized, 73

requirements for naturalization, 68–71
Progressive Era (1901–1914), 166–168
Pronunciation practice, 127–128

Q

Questions, 54–55

R

Ratify, 90
Reading exercises, 11–22
Reading practice, 71–76, 85
Reconstruction (1865–1877), 162–164
Refugee Act of 1980, 13
Representatives, 87, 90
Republic, 78
Rights of citizens, 17–19
Ross, Betsy, 107

S

Secretary of Agriculture, 95
Secretary of Commerce, 95
Secretary of Defense, 95
Secretary of Education, 95
Secretary of Energy, 95
Secretary of Health and Human Services, 95
Secretary of Housing and Urban
    Development, 95
Secretary of Labor, 95
Secretary of State, 95
Secretary of the Interior, 95

Secretary of the Treasury, 95
Secretary of Transportation, 95
Secretary of Veterans' Affairs, 95
Sectional strife and Civil War (1850–1865),
    162
Senators, 88
Separation of powers, 87
Special observances, 104
"Star-Spangled Banner," 107
State government, 99–100
Supreme Court, 87, 98

T

Tripartite system, 89

V

Vice president, 92, 95
Vocabulary words, 197–208

W

Washington, George, 95, 104
Who can be naturalized, 73
Wilson administration (1913–1921),
    168–169
Word list, 197–208
World War I, 168–169
World War II, 172–176
Writing practice, 76
Written English, 68–71

THE UNITED STATES OF AMERICA: *The Present 50 States*

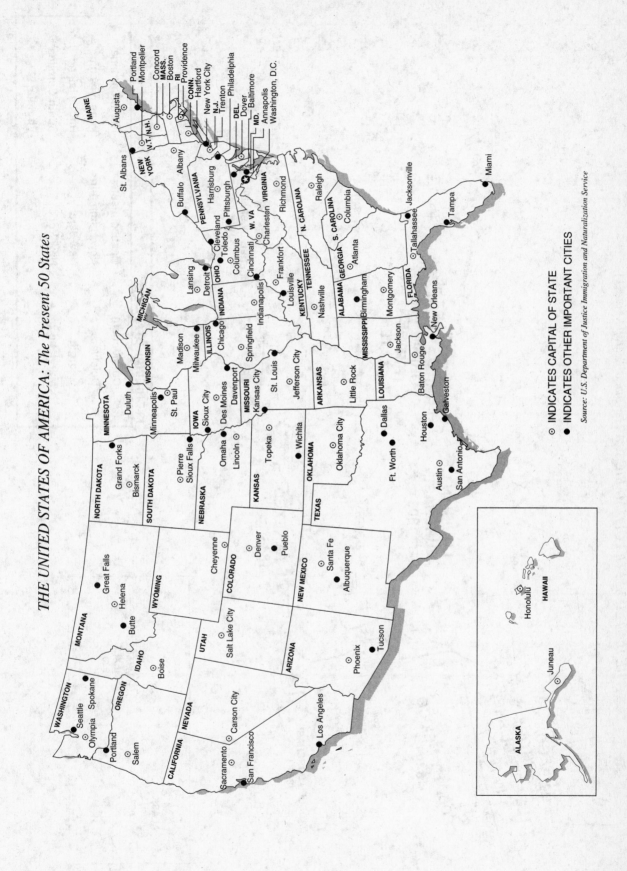

⊙ INDICATES CAPITAL OF STATE

● INDICATES OTHER IMPORTANT CITIES

Source: U.S. Department of Justice Immigration and Naturalization Service

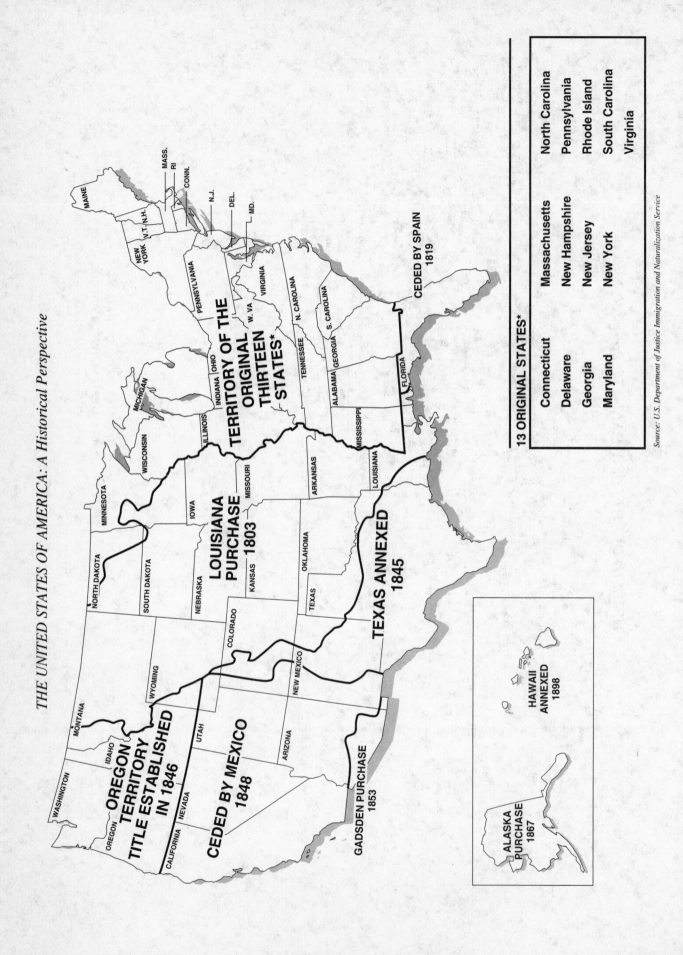

THE UNITED STATES OF AMERICA: A Historical Perspective

13 ORIGINAL STATES*

Connecticut	Massachusetts	North Carolina
Delaware	New Hampshire	Pennsylvania
Georgia	New Jersey	Rhode Island
Maryland	New York	South Carolina
		Virginia

Source: U.S. Department of Justice Immigration and Naturalization Service

NOTES

NOTES

NOTES